THE OFFICE OF
LORD GREAT CHAMBERLAIN OF ENGLAND

AN HISTORICAL AND MODERN STUDY

BY

A.J.M. BAKER, M.A., LL.M., (CANTAB)

First Published in 2005
by A.J.M. BAKER, M.A., LL.M., (CANTAB)

ISBN 0-9551046-0-2

Printed by Barnwell's Print Ltd., Aylsham,
Norfolk NR11 6ET. Tel: 01263 732767

*The Most Hon. David George Philip (7th) Marquess of Cholmondeley in the
uniform of Lord Great Chamberlain and holding his wand of office.*

CONTENTS

FOREWORD BY THE MARQUESS OF CHOLMONDELEY

It may seem surprising that the ancient title of hereditary Lord Great Chamberlain still exists at the beginning of the 21st century. Although the holder of the title no longer has any significant role in the country's affairs, the Lord Great Chamberlain is still the Monarch's representative in the Palace of Westminster, and has specific duties to perform at Coronations, Lyings-in-State and at the Opening of Parliament.

From its creation in the 12th century under King Henry I, the position of Lord Great Chamberlain, held for generations by the de Vere family, once carried considerable power and prestige, though what the incumbent's duties actually were is by no means clear. Certainly by the 18th century his responsibilities were mostly confined to the Palace of Westminster and to officiating on state occasions. At Coronations he would even be expected to help the future Monarch dress for the ceremony, and would sleep the night before in an ajoining chamber.

Responsibility for the running of the Palace of Westminster (or Houses of Parliament) was in the hands of the Lord Great Chamberlain and his offical secretary, The Gentleman Usher of the Blackrod (another ancient title originally linked to the Order of the Garter) until the mid 1960s, when much of the maintenance was taken over by various government committees. Since then, the duties of the Lord Great Chamberlain have been restricted to state occasions although some areas of the Palace are still under his partial control. Day-to-day running of the House of Lords has in fact devolved on Black Rod, who is an appointee of the Lords.

My family came to be hereditary joint holders of the title through a marriage into the Ancaster family in the 1780s. However, as Anthony Baker's most interesting study shows, the correct descent from the de Vere family (the senior line failing in 1625) should have been quite different. Two early rulings, one in the time of King Henry VIII, upheld the wrong line of descent. Then much later, a court ruling at the accession of King Edward VII, following a decision in 1779, pronounced that three families, descendants of the 4th Duke of Ancaster's sisters, should share the position and appoint a deputy to hold the office. The three families agreed to hold the position of deputy in successive reigns, with the Cholmondeley family holding the office in alternate reigns, and the other two families holding the office alternately in the other reigns. This is how the Cholmondeleys come to hold the title under the present Queen.

This is now my responsibility, as Lord Great Chamberlain, to receive the Queen and visiting Heads of State at the Palace of Westminster and carry out the various duties associated with this most historic title.

June 2005   David Cholmondeley

(from photgraph by Deryc R Sands)

Copies of two photographs of The Lord Great Chamberlain receiving the Queen and The Duke of Edinburgh at the entrance to the House of Lords for the State Opening of Parliament.

(from photgraph by Deryc R Sands)

INTRODUCTION

The Lord Great Chamberlainship of England is one of the oldest offices of State that has survived in the descendants of the original holder. It was granted in 1133 to Alberic de Vere and having for centuries been held by the de Vere Earls of Oxford (who subsequently died out) is now held by some of his other descendants, being members or connections of the families of the Marquess of Cholmondeley, Lady Willoughby de Eresby and Lord Carrington. The office is now held (as deputy for all the persons entitled to the office) by David, 7th Marquess of Cholmondeley.

My interest in the office arose through being a partner in the firm of solicitors who acted for the Cholmondeley family and, in particular, through being the solicitor for David's grandfather (the 5th Marquess) in his declining years and his father (the 6th Marquess) until his death in 1990. The 5th, 6th and 7th Marquesses have held the office of Lord Great Chamberlain during the reign of Queen Elizabeth II.

The spur to writing this work was initially reading an article by Geoffrey White on the Office of Lord Great Chamberlain published as Appendix F to Volume X of *The Complete Peerage* and this was followed by my reading *The History of the Lord Great Chamberlainship of England* by Captain G.J. Townsend written in 1934. I was much impressed by the argument of Geoffrey White that for centuries, since the time of King Henry VIII, the office had passed incorrectly and that decisions of the House of Lords as to the persons entitled were incorrect. As a lawyer, I found his argument very convincing but nevertheless the Lords' decisions are binding and hence I set out in this work not only something of his arguments but also the position as it undoubtedly is today.

My other inspiration for this work is the knowledge that it would be approved of by David's grandmother Sybil (whom I knew as Sybil, Dowager Marchioness of Cholmondeley). She, as wife of the 5th Marquess, did a lot of work in the running of the office during the early years of the current reign and in regard to negotiations with the Harold Wilson government as to the future of the office in the 1960s. She was a person for whom I had the utmost respect and felt honoured I could regard her as a friend. It is to her memory that I dedicate this work.

My thanks to David, Marquess of Cholmondeley for his help and support since I first started on the project; indeed he has read through this work and largely improved my punctuation. To Jane, Lady Willoughby de Eresby for her encouragement (and for giving my wife and myself a private showing of Grimsthorpe Castle). The Carrington 'interest' is much more diverse and sorting this out in my own mind (and producing a family tree) was much harder, but I received much help from William Legge-Bourke and Bryan Basset. My apologies for any ommisions or errors in constructing the family trees.

My thanks also to 'Black Rod' (Lt Gen. Sir Michael Willcocks) for help in summarising not only his role but also the current role of the Lord Great Chamberlain. I am also grateful to David's current solicitor, Glenn Hurstfield, and his predecessor, Peter Rainey, for letting me have the files relating to the application made by David to succeed as Lord Great Chamberlain on the death of his father in 1990.

I acknowledge with thanks the permission of Mr Clive Aslet of *Country Life* to quote his article in the *Daily Telegraph* about Westminster Hall. This is set out in Chapter VIII. Also thanks to Lord Cholmondeley, Lady Willoughby de Eresby and Mr William Legge-Bourke for permitting me to make use of the various portraits included in this book.

Finally, my thanks to my wife for her encouragement in the work and to the team at my publishers, Barnwells of Aylsham, Norfolk and my secretary, Mrs Sheila Kidd, for between them sorting out my writing and putting everything in the right form and order.

A. J. M. Baker

CHAPTER I

AN HISTORICAL BACKGROUND

The Lord Great Chamberlainship of England is one of the historic great Offices of State. Indeed, it is recognised as such in the House of Lords Act 1999 which retains the rights of the Earl Marshal and the person holding the office of Lord Great Chamberlain to remain members of the 'reformed' House of Lords and not 'counted' amongst the 90 peers who are elected by their fellow members to remain sitting members of the House. This may be changed on any future alteration to the composition of the House of Lords.

The House of Lords Act 1999 draws a distinction between the Earl Marshal (who is referred to specifically as such) and 'the person holding the office of Lord Great Chamberlain'. This is because only one person is entitled to the office of Earl Marshal (at present the Duke of Norfolk) while the right to the office of Lord Great Chamberlain is held between several people and they have to appoint a deputy as the person to hold the office.

The Lord Great Chamberlain is seen each year at the State Opening of Parliament walking before the Sovereign (and to the Sovereign's left) with the Earl Marshal walking similarly in front of the sovereign. In the past each had to walk backwards but this has recently been changed.

The office of Lord Great Chamberlain was granted by King Henry I in 1133 to Alberic de Vere and his heirs after him. The son of Alberic de Vere was created Earl of Oxford and the office remained with such earls until 1625. There were times between 1133 and 1625 when the office was granted to other persons; these occasions were:

> For 80 years from 1265, on the 5th Earl joining Simon de Montfort in revolt against King Henry III, until it was restored to the 7th Earl in 1345.

> For 97 years from 1388, when the 9th Earl (Duke of Ireland) was attainted, until it was restored to the 13th Earl in 1485.

> For 13 years from 1540, when the 15th Earl died and King Henry VIII gave the office for life elsewhere, until the 16th Earl acted as Lord Great Chamberlain for the coronation of Queen Mary in 1553.

The office is hereditary but can pass to females if there is no direct male heir. However, the right of descent to females is one which passes equally to each of the same degree, whilst with males, the elder 'inherits' in preference to the younger. By the time of the Middle Ages, the rules of inheritance were that if a person had sons, or sons and daughters, the eldest son was the heir, whilst if a person had only daughters, they were equally his heirs (in the technical terms they are 'co parceners').

With most hereditary titles the descent is only to males in a direct line (in this case the technical term is descent to 'heirs male'). The Lord Great Chamberlainship is different in that the original grant was to 'Alberic de Vere and his heirs after him'. This has been construed as a gift to 'heirs general'; if there was no male heir a female (or females) could inherit.

In fact, this principle of descent to females was not recognised on the death of a Lord Great Chamberlain (the 14th Earl of Oxford) in 1526, leaving no children but with three sisters, and the office and the title passed eventually to his cousin (the heir male) and then to his cousin's son, the 15th and 16th Earls of Oxford. (For further details as to how the right to the office passed in 1526, see Appendix D.)

The first time the office passed via a female was in 1625 when the 18th Earl of Oxford died without children. The principle that the office went to the 'heirs general' was accepted and it went via the 18th Earl's aunt to his cousin, Lord Willoughby de Eresby, and remained with this family for seven generations. However, when the great great great grandson of this cousin (who had also inherited the title of Duke of Ancaster) died in 1779, he had no children and no brothers, but two sisters. The question of succession to the Lord Great Chamberlainship was then referred to the House of Lords, who decided these two sisters should hold the office jointly and appoint a deputy to actually act as Lord Great Chamberlain, with the Sovereign having power to appoint such a deputy if the persons entitled to make the appointment failed to agree. At that stage the sisters agreed that the husband of the elder sister should be such deputy.

The elder sister was able to petition to have the Barony of Willoughby de Eresby brought out of abeyance in her favour and the younger sister married the Marquess of Cholmondeley and became Marchioness of Cholmondeley.

For 646 years from 1133, the right to the office of Lord Great Chamberlain had been held by one person, but from 1779 until 1870 it was held equally by the two sisters (or their male descendents); then in 1870 the then Lord Willoughby de Eresby died, leaving only two sisters, so one of the equal half shares was subdivided and each of these two sisters inherited a one quarter share. Again the Barony of Willoughby de Eresby was brought out of abeyance in favour of the elder sister while the younger sister had married Lord Carrington. Thus, from 1870 the then Marquess of Cholmondeley and his heirs were entitled to a one half share and Lady Willoughby de Eresby and her heirs and Lady Carrington and her heirs were each entitled to a one quarter share.

The right to the office became even more complicated in 1928 when the son of Lady Carrington (the Marquess of Lincolnshire) died, with his only son having died from wounds received in the war of 1915. The Marquess had five daughters (who thus each became entitled to a 5 per cent share of the office). There has been a further subdivision since then and the present owners of the office hold the following shares: (see further in chapter V).

> 1 person holds 50%
> 1 person holds 25%
> 3 persons each hold 5%
> 4 persons each hold 1¼%
> 5 persons each hold 1%

Originally, when the two sisters, Lady Willoughby de Eresby and the Marchioness of Cholmondeley, had power to appoint between them a deputy to hold the office of Lord Great Chamberlain, there was disagreement between them after the death in 1820 of the husband of the elder sister (who had become Lord Gwydir and had acted as such deputy). Lady Willoughby de Eresby wished her son, the 2nd Lord Gwydir, to act, while Lady Cholmondeley thought it was the 'turn' of her husband, the 1st Marquess Cholmondeley. The King had to exercise his power to appoint in these circumstance and chose the 2nd Lord Gwydir largely on the basis that Lord Cholmondeley was Lord Steward and therefore should not hold both offices.

Eventually in 1829 it was agreed between the two families that each should act as Lord Great Chamberlain in alternate reigns. The succession was therefore:

The remainder of the reign of George IV	:	The son of Lady Willoughby De Eresby acted as Lord Great Chamberlain.
The reign of William IV	:	The 2nd Marquess of Cholmondeley acted as Lord Great Chamberlain.
The reign of Victoria	:	Successively, the 22nd and 23rd Lords Willoughby de Eresby acted as Lord Great Chamberlain. On the death of the 23rd Lord

Willoughby in 1870 his nephew (who subsequently became the 25th Lord Willoughby) was appointed as deputy by his mother (the 24th Lady Willoughby) and his aunt (Lady Carrington).

Before the end of the reign of Queen Victoria, the Willoughby de Eresby share had split again between the elder branch (which retained the Willoughby de Eresby title) and the younger 'Carrington' branch. So it was agreed (in 1912) that the family of the Marquess of Cholmondeley would retain the right to appoint the deputy in alternate reigns while the Willoughby de Eresby and Carrington families have similar powers in each fourth reign. (See Appendix G for copy of the Deed Poll to give effect to this arrangement.) The succession, therefore, has been:

The reign of Edward VII	: The 4th Marquess of Cholmondeley acted as Lord Great Chamberlain.
The reign of George V	: The then Lord Carrington (who had been created Marquess of Lincolnshire) acted as Lord Great Chamberlain until his death in 1928 when his son-in-law Viscount Lewisham (later the Earl of Dartmouth) was appointed by the Carrington family to succeed him.
The reign of Edward VIII	: The 5th Marquess of Cholmondeley acted as Lord Great Chamberlain.
The reign of George VI	: The 26th Lord Willoughby de Eresby (then Earl of Ancaster) acted as Lord Great Chamberlain until he resigned in favour of his son, the 27th Lord Willoughby de Eresby.
The reign of Elizabeth II	: The 5th Marquess of Cholmondeley acted as Lord Great Chamberlain until he resigned due to failing health, to be succeeded by his son, the 6th Marquess, until his death, when he was succeeded by his son, the 7th (and present) Marquess of Cholmondeley.

Assuming the 1912 agreement is followed (and technically it is not binding as all those who signed it died some years ago and could not bind their successors), in the next reign the Carrington family (being the descendants of the Marquess of Lincolnshire) will nominate the person as the deputy to act as Lord Great Chamberlain, to be succeeded in the next reign by a nominee of the Chomondeley family, to be followed in the next reign by a nominee of the Willoughby de Eresby family.

In each case, the other holders, i.e. the appropriate members of all three families, have to agree and sign the required formal deed. When David, the current (7th) Marquess of Cholmondeley, was appointed by Deed dated 23rd October 1990 to act as deputy Lord Great Chamberlain in place of his father, who died on 13th March 1990, the Deed of Nomination and Appointment (signed in several parts – see Appendix J) had to be signed by 11 people (who between them then shared the office). A similar Deed had to be signed by 11 persons when his father (the 6th Marquess) replaced his grandfather (the 5th Marquess), and a copy of the Deed then executed on 15th March 1966 is shown in Appendix H. If a similar Deed had to be signed now, the number of persons so entitled has increased to 14.

There are two further requirements as to the appointment of such deputy:

1]	The appointment has to be approved by the Sovereign; this would be regarded as a formal matter only, but no doubt the Sovereign would be closely consulted.

2]	The person appointed must not be a person of rank inferior to a knight. It can be noted that of the 14 persons entitled to the office, six are commoners and therefore could not act as deputy.

It can be observed that Lord Chomondeley is not married and has no children, so it is possible his 50 per cent share of the office will eventually pass to his three sisters (two of whom have sons and the third being unmarried). Thus, it is quite possible that in due course the elder son of each of the two married sisters will inherit a 25 per cent share.

Similarly, the current Baroness Willoughby de Eresby is not married and is not likely to have children, and her 25 per cent share of the office will pass via her two aunts to her cousins, Mrs Carola Phillippi and Sir John Aird, each of whom will inherit a 12½ per cent share. Mrs Phillippi has two sons and Sir John has a son, so this inheritance is secure for some time.

It is therefore possible to surmise that by the time another 100 or 200 years have passed, the rights to the office of Lord Great Chamberlain of England will be shared between many people and the present arrangements for rotation of the office will no longer be practical.

CHAPTER II

The History of the Office of Lord Great Chamberlain and the Holders of the Office

Discussion of the history of the Lord Great Chamberlainship is contained in an article by Geoffrey White in Volume X of *The Complete Peerage*, and reference can also be made to the proceedings before the Committee for Privileges of the House of Lords in 1902, and a short history of the office written by Captain C.J. Townsend in the 1930s. The occasion of the 1902 proceedings was to establish who was entitled to the office of the Lord Great Chamberlain, as it was then unclear as to who was entitled to act at the Coronation of King Edward VII.

The persons then claiming the office were the Earl of Ancaster (Lord Willoughby de Eresby), solely on his own behalf; the Marquess of Cholmondeley and the Earl Carrington (who claimed to hold the office jointly with the Earl of Ancaster); the Duke of Atholl, who claimed the office as being the true heir general of Alberic de Vere or alternatively as the true heir general of the 17th Earl of Oxford; and the Attorney General on behalf of the Crown, whose main argument was that the right to claim for the office had lapsed when the 14th Earl of Oxford died in 1526 leaving no issue but three sisters.

There is no dispute in respect of the position from 1133 until the death of the 14th Earl of Oxford in 1526, as the right to the office had descended from Alberic de Vere to his son, created 1st Earl of Oxford, and then to successive Earls of Oxford as heirs general; although there had been occasions when the Earl was in conflict with the Crown or had been attainted and the office was given to other persons. The last instance of the reversal of an attainder was in 1485 when the 13th Earl of Oxford recovered the office of Lord Great Chamberlain and acted as such at the coronation of King Henry VII, and subsequently the coronation of his wife Elizabeth of York as Queen and the coronation of King Henry VIII. On his death, the office passed to his nephew and heir general, the 14th Earl.

It was on the death of the 14th Earl, leaving three sisters, that the problems arose. The argument before the Committee for Privileges of the House of Lords in 1902 shows that three possibilities had to be considered.

1) The right passed to the eldest of the three sisters (*the Droit d'Ainesse*) in accordance with the law at it would have been understood in 1133 and for two centuries or so thereafter. This was the basis for the first claim of the Duke of Atholl who was descended from the eldest sister.

2)   Since there was no single claimant but there were three females equally entitled, either the right lapsed to the Crown or went into abeyance until there was a single claimant (this was the basis of the Crown's claim).

3)   The position had been established by an award of the King in 1531/32 to settle a dispute between the new 15th Earl of Oxford and his cousins, the three sisters of the 14th Earl. (See Appendix D for details.)

Whilst King Henry VIII did in his lifetime (after the death of the 15th Earl) appoint the right to the office elsewhere, it was recovered by the 16th Earl for the coronations of Queen Mary and Queen Elizabeth I and passed to his son and grandson, the 17th and 18th Earls.

The right of such Earls to the office can only be based on the award of King Henry VIII confirmed by Act of Parliament (see Appendix D), and whilst Geoffrey White convincingly argues that this view cannot be supported, it has been accepted ever since. The position was clearly set out in the judgement of the Lord Chancellor to the Committee for Privileges of 6th May 1902:

> *The primary question for the Committee is whether the office passed to the Earl of Oxford by the award of King Henry VIII and the Act of Parliament confirming the award. Now it must be observed that these documents are capable of bearing the construction that the office passed, and they have received that construction for upwards of three centuries, both in practice and by a resolution of this House. I think, therefore, that the Committee will be justified in declining to consider the construction de novo.*

The next confusion arose on the death of the 18th Earl in 1625. The Earl had three half-sisters but the title of Earl of Oxford went to a second cousin as 19th Earl. However, the 17th Earl had a sister (of the full blood), and her son Lord Willoughby de Eresby successfully claimed the office on the basis that he was the heir general of the 18th Earl as being the nearest relative of the whole blood and hence, as the law was then understood in relation to this case, took precedence over the three sisters of the 18th Earl who were only of the half blood (being daughters of a previous marriage of the 17th Earl). The alternative claim by the Duke of Atholl in 1902 was on the basis that this decision was wrong and he was entitled as senior heir of the sisters of half blood.

The position was reviewed in 1660/61 for the coronation of King Charles II but although other claimants put in their claims, none were pursued in the House of Lords and the then Lord Willoughby de Eresby (also then Earl of Lindsey) was confirmed in the office. The right to the office then passed for the next five generations from father to son until 1779 when the then Lord Willoughby de Eresby (then Duke of Ancaster) died leaving two sisters as his heirs.

Petitions to exercise the rights of the office were presented by the elder sister Priscilla (who became Lady Willoughby de Eresby) in her right by her husband Mr Peter Burrell as senior co-heir, and by the new Duke of Ancaster as heir male. Initially the Attorney General decided that Mr Burrell was entitled to act as Lord Great Chamberlain in the right of his wife, but the matter was then referred to the House of Lords. Further claims were made by Lord Percy (later Duke of Northumberland) as senior co-heir of Lady Latimer, eldest sister of the 14th Earl of Oxford, and by the Dowager Duchess of Atholl as heir general of the Countess of Derby, eldest sister of the half blood of the 18th Earl of Oxford.

The House of Lords having heard evidence from counsel referred two questions to the Judges. The first question was whether the claims of Lord Percy and the Dowager Duchess of Atholl were barred by lapse of time. The Judges decided such claims were so barred, 'there having been adverse possession of more than 60 years…..(the) right would be barred in any real action by the Statue of Limitations.'

The second question put to the Judges was 'Does the said office belong to the eldest (co-heiress) alone or to both; or in either case is the husband of the eldest entitled to execute the said office or may both sisters execute the office by deputy, and how must such deputy be appointed.' Seemingly the House of Lords had decided, before submitting such question, that the claim of the Duke of Ancaster as heir male was invalid against the claims on behalf of the joint heirs general. The Judges answered the question as follows:

1] That the Office of Lord Great Chamberlain belongs to both sisters.
2] That the husband of the eldest is not of right entitled to execute it.
3] That both the sisters may execute it by deputy to be appointed by them.
4] Such deputy not being of a degree inferior to a Knight.
5] And to be approved by the King.

There are two somewhat surprising factors about the decision. First, no claim had been made or argued on behalf of the younger sister (then unmarried) but she benefited by the decision. Secondly, the second question was never argued before the Judges by counsel, who gave their opinion without argument, and then the House of Lords adopted their opinion verbatim without further argument.

As a result of this decision, the two sisters appointed Mr Burrell (who had been knighted) as their deputy. He was subsequently advanced by being given the title of Lord Gwydir and held the office (as deputy) until his death in 1820. As set out in the previous chapter the sisters could not agree on his successor so the King himself appointed the son of Lord Gwydir (the 2nd Baron) as deputy. Then in 1829 the sisters came to the agreement that they would each nominate a deputy in alternate reigns. The 2nd Lord Gwydir (later succeeding his mother as 22nd Lord Willoughby de Eresby) acted as deputy in the reign of King George IV, the Marquess of Cholomondeley acted as deputy in the reign of King William IV and successive Lords Willoughby de Eresby acted as deputies in the reign of Queen Victoria.

As already described, by the time of the death of Queen Victoria, the interest of the Willoughby de Eresby family had been split again with the death of the 23rd Lord Willoughby de Eresby in 1870, leaving two sisters. Of the two sisters, the elder, Lady Aveland, had the benefit of the Willoughby de Eresby title being taken out of abeyance in her favour, while the younger sister married and became Lady Carrington. Each sister, therefore, had a one quarter share in the office of Lord Great Chamberlain, the Marquess of Cholmondeley, of course, retaining the other half share.

In the reign of King Edward VII and following the House of Lords 1902 decision (see appendix E), the 4th Marquess of Cholmondeley acted as deputy Lord Great Chamberlain. In 1912 the three then holders of the office executed a new Deed Poll agreeing the office should rotate by successive reigns (see Appendix G for copy of the Deed Poll); the Marquess of Cholmondeley and his heirs acting in alternate reigns, Lord Willoughby de Eresby and his heirs in every fourth reign, and Lord Carrington and his heirs in every fourth reign.

It was the turn of the Carrington interest to act as deputy Lord Great Chamberlain during the reign of King George V. The first of the Carrington holders of the office was the son of Lady Carrington (who became Marquess of Lincolnshire), and on his death in 1928, leaving five daughters (his only son, Viscount Wendover, having been killed in the Great War), one of his sons-in-law, Viscount Lewisham, held the office for the remainder of the reign of King George V. The office reverted to the 5th Marquess of Cholmondeley for the short reign of King Edward VIII and then went back to the 26th Lord Willoughby de Eresby (then 2nd Earl of Ancaster) for the reign of King George VI. However, the 26th Lord

Willoughby de Eresby retired as deputy shortly before the death of King George VI to be replaced by his son, later the 27th Lord Willoughby de Eresby (3rd Earl of Ancaster).   For the reign of Queen Elizabeth II, the 5th Marquess of Cholmondeley acted as deputy Lord Great Chamberlain (as he had for the reign of King Edward VIII) until he retired in favour of his son (then Earl of Rocksavage, subsequently 6th Marquess of Cholmondeley). On the death of the 6th Marquess of Cholmondeley, the office passed to his son David (the 7th and present Marquess of Cholmondeley) who now holds the office (a copy of the Deed executed in several parts and signed by all persons then entitled to the office nominating and appointing him as their deputy is included as Appendix J).

CHAPTER III

A Brief History of the Earls of Oxford (1147-1703) and the Periods when they held the Office of Lord Great Chamberlain

The office of Lord Great Chamberlain was awarded to Alberic de Vere (Aubrey de Vere) and his heirs in 1133. His father (also Aubrey de Vere) was one of the knights who was in William the Conqueror's army at the Battle of Hastings in 1066. It is believed he came from Ver in the Cotentin in France, hence his name was spelt in his time 'de Ver'. He was clearly a prominent figure since after the conquest he was given lands in Essex, Suffolk, Cambridgeshire and elsewhere (including Kensington). He established a residence at Hedingham in Essex and this, in time, became the family's principal seat (Castle Hedingham).

His son Aubrey de Vere clearly stood in royal favour with King Henry I, serving as sheriff of several counties and being appointed Master Chamberlain (Lord Great Chamberlain) in July 1133. He was well connected and had several children. One son (William) was the nominee of Empress Maud to be Chancellor of England, and one daughter (Juliana) married the Earl of Norfolk. His children lived in troubled times and his eldest son Aubrey, who followed as Lord Great Chamberlain, at times supported the Empress Maud's claims to the throne and at times made his peace with King Stephen. It was the Empress who granted him the title of Earl of Oxford by 1147. Originally it was suggested that the title should be Earl of Cambridgshire, but the King of Scots believed this title to be part of his Earldom of Huntingdon so the title of Oxford replaced that of Cambridge! He not only lived in troubled times but had a troubled matrimonial history, being married three times. His first wife was a French countess, so for a time he was 'Count of Guisnes', but when the marriage broke up he had to give up this title. His second wife died, and his third wife (Agnes) was very young at her marriage. Problems soon arose in this marriage and eventually Agnes obtained an order from the Pope to her husband to make him take her back as wife. This obviously worked as they had seven children. The Earl survived into the reign of King Richard I and had to contribute £30.2s 6d to the King's ransom after the Crusade.

Two sons of the 1st Earl succeeded each other as Earls of Oxford and had to live through the problems of the reign of King John. Indeed, it is believed Aubrey, the 2nd Earl, acted as Lord Great Chamberlain at the coronation of King John. He died in the lifetime of King John and his brother, Robert, succeeded as 3rd Earl. He was one of the 'Barons' who signed the Magna Carta and one of the 25 elected as its guardians. In this role, he took arms against the King and invited

Louis, son of the King of France, to take the throne. For a time he alternated his loyalty but with the death of King John in 1216 he finally reverted to supporting the new young English king (Henry III), in 1217. He was restored to his property the next year and probably acted as Lord Great Chamberlain at King Henry's second crowning in 1220. The Earl died the next year.

His son Hugh, the 4th Earl, held the office of Lord Great Chamberlain for a large part of King Henry III's reign and acted as the King's Chamberlain at the coronation of his wife, Queen Eleanor, in 1236 and the next year went on a pilgrimage 'beyond the seas'. He continued his father's role in seeking to enforce the provisions of the Magna Carta, becoming, from 1258, a member of the Committee of 24 and from the next year, of the smaller Committee of 12, both of which were established under the Provisions of Oxford in 1258. The Earl died in 1263 as civil war (which had threatened since 1258) broke out.

His son, the new (5th) Earl, was closely allied to Simon de Montfort in the civil war, being knighted by him preceding the Battle of Lewes. He was, however, captured at Kenilworth, losing his title and the Lord Great Chamberlainship as a result. He later recovered the Earldom but not the Lord Great Chamberlainship. The recovery of the title was by arrangement with Roger Mortimer, Earl of March (who had been granted the Oxford title) on the 5th Earl agreeing to the marriage of his son with Mortimer's daughter. Both the 5th Earl and his son the 6th Earl served in wars against the Welsh and Scots and sought to recover the office of Lord Great Chamberlain but were unsuccessful in this. John, the 7th Earl (who was a nephew of the 6th Earl), was more fortunate and recovered the office in 1345. He fought in several military campaigns and was one of the commanders of the 1st Division at both the battles of Crecy and Poitiers. He was eventually killed whilst besieging Rheims in 1360. His son Thomas, the 8th Earl, continued in much the same way as his father but only held the title for 12 years before he died in 1371, leaving as his only son Robert, the 9th Earl, aged 11.

The 9th Earl was fortunate in that he was brought up often in the company of Richard, the son of the Black Prince, who, after the Prince's death, was the heir of his grandfather (King Edward III) and on his death succeeded as King Richard II. Not surprisingly, the friendship continued and the young Earl acted as Lord Great Chamberlain at the coronation in 1377, although still a minor. He was also at the new King's side when he faced Wat Tyler and his rebels at Mile End, London, in 1381. It seemed prudent to the King to confirm to Robert the original grant of the office to Aubrey de Vere and his heirs (in 1133), and this he did by further charter in 1382 (see

Appendix D). Having served with the King against the Scots, there were then problems in Ireland and the King sent the young Earl to Ireland in 1385 to rule this country on his behalf. The Earl in 1385 was advanced to the title of Marquis of Dublin but this was revoked the next year as he was then created Duke of Ireland (the title was the first non-royal duke created).

His advancement not surprisingly incited jealousy and perhaps matrimonial problems exacerbated matters. Richard was forced to abandon his friend (who was to face a charge of treason), but helped him to escape. The Duke (9th Earl) then raised troops in the north-west and advanced on London. He was met by troops of the Earl of Arundel and Earl of Derby (later King Henry IV) and was defeated beside the Thames at the Battle of Radcot Bridge (1388). He escaped to France and then to Belgium but died in a hunting accident in 1392 leaving no children. Having been declared guilty of treason by the 'Merciless' Parliament of 1388 he had lost his Dukedom, Earldom and the Lord Great Chamberlainship.

There now commenced a significant period when the Lord Great Chamberlainship was not held by the Earls of Oxford but by other peers for life. Indeed, it was 97 years before it was restored to the 13th Earl in 1485.

It is interesting to note that one of the persons who held the office during this interim period (from 1450 to 1460) was John 1st Viscount Beaumont (descended from a daughter of the 7th Earl of Oxford). His mother was a daughter of the 5th Lord Willoughby de Eresby, so there was an early connection of the office with the title of Lord Willoughby de Eresby.

The 9th Earl's uncle, Aubrey de Vere, had served the Crown well, having been Secretary to the Black Prince, Chamberlain (as opposed to Lord Great Chamberlain) of the Royal Household, and was with King Richard and the 9th Earl when they met Wat Tyler and the rebels. On the 9th Earl being found guilty of treason he lost his offices and power but on the 9th Earl's death childless, he was the heir and recovered first the entailed estates and then the Earldom, in 1393. He attempted to recover the Lord Great Chamberlainship but was unsuccessful. He made a further attempt for the coronation of King Henry IV (1399) but failed yet again and died the next year (1400).

His son Richard became 11th Earl. He distinguished himself as one of King Henry V's commanders at the siege of Harfleur and the Battle of Agincourt. He was made a Knight of the Garter in 1416 (as the 9th Earl had been) but died the same year.

The next Earl was his son John, the 12th Earl, who succeeded to the title at the age of eight. He was unfortunate to live during the early part of the Wars of the Roses. Although he served for a time under the Duke of York, he was in fact a Lancastrian and intended to fight as such at the first battle of St Albans. Unfortunately, he arrived too late to take part in the battle (1455), which was won by the Yorkists, who at that time took control of the country but did not dethrone King Henry VI. For the next six years he took little part in national affairs. He was no doubt pleased at the Yorkist defeat and the death of the Duke of York at the battle of Wakefield (1460), and a further Yorkist defeat at the second battle of St Albans (1461), but then heard of the Yorkist success at Towton (1461) under the Duke of York's son, the new King Edward IV. Within a year the Earl and his eldest son were accused of plotting against the new King and condemned to death, the son being executed six days before his father, hence never inheriting the title.

The Earl's second son John (who was just under age at the time of his father's and brother's executions) was allowed to succeed to the title as 13th Earl, and indeed acted as temporary Great Chamberlain at the coronation of Queen Elizabeth Woodville in 1465. He was, however, three years later committed to the Tower on suspicion of plotting, but pardoned soon afterwards (1469). A year later he joined the Lancastrian Queen Margaret in France and was with her when she reclaimed the throne for her husband. He was appointed Constable and as such condemned to death the Earl of Worcester, who had similarly condemned his father and brother to death. On King Edward IV's returning to the country, the Earl led the Lancastrian right wing at the Battle of Barnet, where he had some success until some misunderstandings in the fog led to a Lancastrian defeat. He escaped to Scotland and later made an unsuccessful attempt at landing in Essex, and subsequently held St Michael's Mount in Cornwall for some time. From there he was imprisoned in Calais in France (in the part held by England), but escaped in 1485 to join Henry Tudor in his invasion to claim the throne. He was one of Henry Tudor's principal commanders and played a significant role in the Battle of Bosworth, commanding the main attacking force.

Not surprisingly, he was in high favour with the new King Henry VII and his attainder (made in 1475) was reversed in 1485; he was restored to his estates, and became Lord High Admiral and Knight of the Garter. The office of Lord Great Chamberlain was confirmed to him (see Appendix D) and he officiated at the coronation of King Henry VII and his wife Queen Elizabeth of York, and later at the coronation of King Henry VIII. He was a witness to many charters of King Henry VII, being described therein as 'our very dear kinsman John, Earl of Oxford, Great Chamberlain of England'.

The 13th Earl died in 1513 to be succeeded by his nephew John, the 14th Earl, then aged 14. He was in the wardship of the Duke of Norfolk (who acted as Lord Great Chamberlain during his minority) and married his daughter, but was still kept under the control of his father-in-law after he came of age due to his extravagance.

It was with the death of the 14th Earl in 1526 that direct descent of the Lord Great Chamberlainship to the heirs general of the original Alberic de Vere came to an end. He left three sisters who were his heirs general, but by the award of King Henry VIII his 'offices' went to the new Earl, his second cousin (another John), who was a great grandson of the 11th Earl. It was subsequently decided that the word 'offices' included the Lord Great Chamberlainship, but clearly this was not the view of the King, who had already awarded the office to the new Earl, but only for life. The 15th Earl was an established figure at Court and bore the crown at Queen Anne Boleyn's coronation, having been a commissioner for the deposition of Queen Catherine of Aragon. He was then one of the peers who tried Queen Anne in 1536, and the next year attended the funeral of Queen Jane Seymour. He died in 1540, when King Henry VIII awarded the Lord Great Chamberlainship elsewhere, and indeed during the remaining years of his reign made five different appointments for life of the office.

The 15th Earl was succeeded by his son, the 16th Earl, who made attempts to recover the Lord Great Chamberlainship, but was instead ordered in 1547 to surrender the patent of the office. Nevertheless, on the death of King Edward VI he initially supported Lady Jane Grey as Queen, but changed to Queen Mary and then acted as Lord Great Chamberlain at her coronation. At the coronation of Queen Elizabeth he petitioned (as of right) to act as Lord Great Chamberlain and this petition was granted, so the right to the office was recovered by the new Earl. On his death in 1562 the office passed to his son, Edward, the 17th Earl.

Edward, the 17th Earl, was a noted man of letters and playwright (thought by some to have written some or all of the plays ascribed to William Shakespeare). He had a difficult relationship with his first wife, the daughter of the Lord Treasurer, William Cecil Lord Burghley, by whom he had three daughters. He was an established and extravagant man at Queen Elizabeth's court although, like others, he fell from favour from time to time. He survived the Queen and acted as Lord Great Chamberlain at the coronation of King James I, but died the next year (1604).

His heir was his only son, Henry, son of his second wife, who succeeded as 18th Earl aged 11. He was somewhat freespoken and his criticism of government led to 18 months imprisonment. He was abroad for some time and died in 1625 from wounds received at the siege of Breda. His death was shortly after the death of King James I, and as he left no son there was an immediate problem as to who was entitled to act as Lord Great Chamberlain at the coronation of King Charles I. In fact, no final decision had been made by the time of the coronation and the Earl of Worcester acted then in a temporary capacity. Later that year, it was held by the House of Lords, on advice from a majority of five leading judges, that his second cousin, Robert de Vere, was entitled to the Earldom as heir male, but not to the Lord Great Chamberlainship which passed to his first cousin, Lord Willoughby de Eresby, as heir general. It was decided he was the true heir general, being of the whole blood (son of a sister of the 17th Earl), rather than the 18th Earl's step-sisters (daughters of the 17th Earl by his first marriage to Anne Cecil).

The second cousin, Robert, succeeded as 19th Earl with no great fortune at his disposal. He also served abroad (under another cousin, Lord Vere of Tilbury). He married a Dutch lady but was killed at the siege of Maastricht in 1632.

His son Aubrey, the 20th and last Earl of Oxford, held the title for 71 years. His early years were the years of the Civil War but he came to the fore thereafter bearing the sword 'Curtana' at the coronation of King Charles II, and the Sword of State at the coronation of King James II, King William III and Queen Anne. He died in 1703 and his only son had died in infancy but he left four daughters. The only one to marry married the 1st Duke of St Albans (illegitimate son of King Charles II) and from her the later Dukes of St Albans are descended.

The 20th Earl was the only remaining 'heir male' of the 1st Earl and with his death the title became extinct.

CHAPTER IV

The Lord Great Chamberlains from 1625 until the Present Day.

This chapter only gives brief details of the persons who held the office of Lord Great Chamberlain in their own right or as deputy for the co-holders of the office. Fuller details of some of such persons are set out in Captain Townsend's *History of the Great Chamberlainship of England* (1934).

On the death of the 18th Earl of Oxford it was held that his heir general was his aunt (Mary de Vere), the sister of his father, the 17th Earl, rather than his own half-sisters (who were the three children of the 17th Earl's first marriage). Mary de Vere had married the 13th Lord Willoughby de Eresby and it was her son, Robert, having succeeded as 14th Lord Willoughby de Eresby, who successfully claimed the Lord Great Chamberlainship in 1626. His father had been a noted diplomat and soldier in the reign of Queen Elizabeth I and was commander of the English forces helping the Netherlands against the Spaniards in the late 1580s. Later he commanded the small forces sent to help Henry of Navarre succeed as King Henry IV of France. Whilst the 14th Lord Willoughby de Eresby was also a recognised soldier of some achievement, and, as can be seen, came from a notable family, his success in claiming the Lord Great Chamberlainship and his immediate advancement to the Earldom of Lindsey in 1626 was probably partly due to his father's achievements and partly due to his position as Lord Great Chamberlain, so that he was of the same rank as the Earls of Oxford who had previously held the office.

He was Admiral and Governor of the Fleet at the siege of La Rochelle in 1628, and being a firm royalist he was a General in the Royal forces in the Civil War, but was wounded at the Battle of Edgehill in 1642 and died a prisoner the next day.

For the next six generations the office of Lord Great Chamberlain passed in direct male line to the succeeding Earls of Lindsey and in fact, the holder of the Earldom (the 4th Earl and 17th Lord Willoughby de Eresby) was advanced to the Dukedom of Ancaster in 1715.

Of the six generations, the 15th Lord Willoughby (the 2nd Earl of Lindsey) fought with his father at the Battle of Edgehill and like him was taken prisoner. After his release, he rejoined the Cavalier army and was wounded at the Battle of Naseby. He was a consistent Royalist and was one of the earls who arranged the burial of King Charles I after his execution. On the Restoration, he was made a Privy Councillor and acted as Lord Great Chamberlain at the coronation of King Charles II.

The 16th Lord Willoughby (3rd Earl of Lindsey) succeeded his father in 1666 as Lord Great Chamberlain and also became a privy councillor He died in 1701 to be succeeded by his son, the 17th Lord Willoughby (4th Earl of Lindsey) who (having previously been created Marquess of Lindsey by Queen Anne) was created Duke of Ancaster in 1715 shortly after the accession of King George I. As Earl, the 1st Duke was a prominent member of the Whig Party, the main supporters of King George I. The advancement of the Earl from the Marquessate to the Dukedom was to reward the Whig Party, and in particular to gain support in Lincolnshire. The 1st Duke's son, the 18th Lord Willoughby (2nd Duke of Ancaster), acted as Lord Great Chamberlain at the coronation of King George II, while his son, the 19th Lord Willoughby (3rd Duke of Ancaster), acted as Lord Great Chamberlain at the coronation of King George III. Having raised a regiment of soldiers for the King (George II) at the time of the 1745 Jacobite Rebellion, he remained involved with the army, becoming a General in 1772. He was also made Master of the Horse in 1766.

The 19th Lord Willoughby died in 1778 and his only son (the 20th Lord Willoughby and 4th Duke of Ancaster) only survived him for one year and it was on his death in 1779 that the office of Lord Great Chamberlain became divided between his two sisters. The Dukedom passed to his uncle (brother of the 3rd Duke), but as he was childless, it became extinct on his death in 1809, as did the Marquessate and Earldom of Lindsey. The elder of the two sisters of the 4th Duke was able to petition to take the Barony of Willoughby de Eresby out of abeyance, and became the 21st holder of the Barony.

As explained in other chapters, on it being established (in 1781) that the two sisters of the 4th Duke of Ancaster were entitled as co-holders of the office of Lord Great Chamberlain to appoint a deputy to act for them, the husband of the elder sister (Mr Peter Burrell) was appointed as such deputy. He had been an M.P. and was elected one again from 1782 to 1796, and was knighted on 6th July 1781 so that he should be of sufficient 'quality' to act as deputy. He acted as Lord Great Chamberlain for the trial (1788 to 1795) in the House of Lords of Warren Hastings, Governor General of India. He succeeded to a great uncle's baronetcy and was himself given a peerage (as Lord Gwydir) in 1796.

On his death in 1820 there was disagreement between the two sisters (Lady Willoughby de Eresby and the Marchioness of Cholmondeley) as to who should be appointed as their deputy and eventually the King (George IV) nominated the son of Lord Gwydir and Lady Willoughby de Eresby and the two sisters had to acquiesce. He acted as deputy for the remainder of the reign of King George IV, but in accordance with the agreement between the two families stood down for the reign of King William IV.

The person who acted as deputy for the reign of King William IV was George, 2nd Marquess of Cholmondeley (the elder son of the younger sister of the 4th Duke of Ancaster). He also had been an M.P. and later became a Privy Councillor.

On the death of King William IV, in accordance with the family agreement, for the reign of Queen Victoria the 2nd Lord Gwydir (by then the 22nd Lord Willoughby de Eresby) returned as deputy and continued to act as Lord Great Chamberlain until his death in 1865. On his death, he was succeeded as deputy by his son Alberic who became the 23rd Lord Willoughby de Eresby, but he only survived his father by five years, dying in 1870, leaving no son but two sisters. Of these two sisters the elder, Dowager Lady Aveland, became the 24th Lady Willoughby de Eresby (on the Barony being taken out of abeyance in her favour) whilst the younger was Lady Carrington. The two sisters appointed the son of the elder (then Lord Aveland, subsequently the 25th Lord Willoughby de Eresby and later Earl of Ancaster), as deputy and he continued as such until the death of Queen Victoria in 1901.

It was on the death of Queen Victoria that the issue as to how the Lord Great Chamberlainship devolved was questioned again and argued before the Committee for Privileges of the House of Lords. In the meantime, the new King Edward VII had nominated the 4th Marquess of Cholmondeley to act in the interim as Lord Great Chamberlain at his coronation. The House of Lords eventually decided that the office was held between the three families: Lord Cholmondeley owning a half, Lord Willoughby de Eresby (Earl of Ancaster) one quarter, and Lord Carrington one quarter. In accordance with a new family agreement (and consistent with the previous family agreement), Lord Cholmondeley acted as deputy for the whole of the reign of King Edward VII.

On the death of King Edward VII it was the turn of the holder of the Carrington interest to act as deputy. The then Lord Carrington was a distinquished person who had already acted as Lord Chamberlain of Queen Victoria's household from 1892 to 1895, and was previously Governor General of New South Wales (1855-1890); he was also President of the Board of Agriculture and Fisheries (1905-1911) and Lord Privy Seal (1911-1912). Having been created an Earl, he was advanced to the Marquessate of Lincolnshire in 1912. He acted as Lord Great Chamberlain for the coronation and most of the reign of King George V but died in 1928. He had been greatly saddened by the death of his only son, Viscount Wendover, of wounds received in the First World War in 1915. The Marquess of Lincolnshire was survived by five daughters, and the husband of one of them, Viscount Lewisham (heir of the Earl of Dartmouth), was nominated to act as Lord Great Chamberlain until the end of the reign of King George V.

For the brief reign of King Edward VIII it was the turn of the 5th Marquess of Cholmondeley to act as Lord Great Chamberlain but such was the short nature of the reign, with the King abdicating before his projected coronation, that the services Lord Cholmondeley had to give were correspondingly few.

For the reign of King George VI the office went back to the Willoughby de Eresby family and Gilbert, 2nd Earl of Ancaster and 26th Lord Willoughby de Eresby (the son of the 1st Earl, who had been Lord Great Chamberlain in the declining years of Queen Victoria) became Lord Great Chamberlain and acted as such at the King's coronation and during the war years. He died in 1951, but shortly before his death he had (in 1950) resigned as Lord Great Chamberlain and his son (who, on his fathers death, succeeded as the 3rd Earl of Ancaster and 27th Lord Willoughby de Eresby) continued as Lord Great Chamberlain until the King's death in 1952.

The 5th Marquess of Cholmondeley, disappointed at losing the chance to act as Lord Great Chamberlain at the coronation of King Edward VIII (which never took place), was able to act as such at the coronation of Queen Elizabeth II in 1953. He continued as Lord Great Chamberlain to see through the reorganisation that took place during the Harold Wilson government (see Chapter VII), but due to declining health, resigned the office in 1968 so his son the 6th Marquess could succeed him. The 6th Marquess (who had won an M.C. during the Second World War) acted as Lord Great Chamberlain (during his father's remaining lifetime under his courtesy title of Earl of Rocksavage) until his death in 1990 when he was succeeded by his son David, the 7th and current Marquess of Cholmondeley. Hopefully he will continue as Lord Great Chamberlain for the remainder of the current reign of Queen Elizabeth II but on her death should be succeeded by a nominee from the Carrington family for the next reign.

Robert, 1st Earl of Lindsey (14th Baron Willoughby de Eresby) K.G. Lord Great Chamberlain 1626 - 1642.

(copy of a painting by Cornelius Johnson)

Robert 14th Baron Willoughby de Eresby as a grandson of the 16th Earl of Oxford was the successful claimant to the office of Lord Great Chamberlain on the death of the 18th Earl of Oxford in 1626.   He was created Earl of Lindsey that year. Both he and his son were firm Royalists during the Civil War and fought at the Battle of Edgehill, where the 1st Earl received wounds from which he died the next day.   The 2nd Earl was nominal Lord Great Chamberlain, but could not act as such during the Commonwealth.   On the restoration of Charles II he was able to perform his duties and acted as Lord Great Chamberlain at his coronation.

Montagu, 2nd Earl of Lindsey (15th Baron Willoughby de Eresby) K.G. Lord Great Chamberlain 1642 - 1666.

(from copy made in the 19th century from original painting ascribed to Van Dyck)

*Robert 3rd Earl of
Lindsey (16th Baron
Willoughby de Eresby)
Lord Great
Chamberlain
1666 - 1701.*

(copy of a painting by Sir Peter Lely)

*Robert 1st Duke of Ancaster
and 4th Earl of Lindsey. (17th
Baron Willoughby de Eresby)
Lord Great Chamberlain
1701 - 1723*

(copy of a painting by Sir Godfrey Kneller)

Peregrine 2nd Duke of Ancaster and 5th Earl of Lindsey (18th Baron Willoughby de Eresby) Lord Great Chamberlain 1723 - 1742

(copy of a painting from school of Sir G. Kneller)

Peregrine 3rd Duke of Ancaster and 6th Earl of Lindsey (19th Baron Willoughby de Eresby) Lord Great Chamberlain 1742 - 1778.

(copy of a painting by Andrea Casali)

Two pictures showing the three children of the 3rd Duke of Ancaster. The one below shows his son (who became 4th Duke of Ancaster and 20th Baron Willoughby de Eresby) with the younger of his two sisters Georgiana (who subsequently married the 1st Marquess of Cholmondeley). The picture on the right shows Priscilla, the elder of the two sisters (she married Peter Burrell who was later created 1st Lord Gwydir). The 4th Duke died only one year after his father but was Lord Great Chamberlain for that one year.

(copy of a painting by Sir Joshua Reynolds)

The barony of Willoughby de Eresby went into abeyance on the death of the 4th Duke but Priscilla petitioned for it to be taken out of abeyance in her favour and hence became the 21st Baroness Willoughby de Eresby.

The decision of the House of Lords was that the office of Lord Great Chamberlain passed equally to both sisters and it was agreed the husband of the elder (Lord Gwydir) should act as their deputy and hold the office of Lord Great Chamberlain, which he did until his death in 1820.

(copy of a painting by Richard Cosway)

Peter Robert 22nd Baron Willoughby de Eresby, 2nd Lord Gwydir, Lord Great Chamberlain 1820 until the death of George IV in 1830 and then again on the accession of Queen Victoria in 1837 until his own death in 1865.

(copy of a painting by Sir George Hayter)

George Horatio 2nd Marquess of Cholmondeley. Lord Great Chamberlain during the reign of William IV 1830 - 1837.

(copy of a painting by C T Thompson)

Alberic, 23rd Baron Willoughby de Eresby, 3rd Lord of Gwydir, Lord Great Chamberlain 1865-1870.

(copy of sculpture by Lawrence McDonald)

Sir Gilbert Henry Heathcote 6th Baronet, 2nd Baron Aveland. On the death of his mother the Dowager Lady Aveland (24th Baroness Willoughby de Eresby) 1888 he became 25th Baron Willoughby de Eresby. Created Earl of Ancaster 1892 Lord Great Chamberlain 1870-1901

copy of a painting by J. Hanson Walker 1881

George Henry Hugh 4th
Marquess of Cholmondeley
Lord Great Chamberlain
during the reign of Edward VII
1901 - 1911

Charles Robert Marquess of
Lincolnshire
Lord Great Chamberlain from
1911 for the early part of the
reign of George V. On his
death in 1928 he was
succeeded by his son-in-law
William Viscount Lewisham
until the death of George V in
1936.

Sir Gilbert 2nd Earl of Ancaster, 26th Baron Willoughby de Eresby and 3rd Lord Aveland G.C.V.O.

(copy of a painting by Sir Arthur Cope)

The 2nd Earl of Ancaster and his son the 3rd Earl acted as Lord Great Chamberlain during the reign of King George VI. The 2nd Earl so acted from the accession of King George VI in 1936 until, due to failing health, he resigned in favour of his son in 1950. His son (known as James) an MP was created Sir Gilbert Heathcote in his own right in order to carry out the duties of Lord Great Chamberlain which he did for the remainder of the reign of King George VI (who died in 1952). He succeeded his father in 1951 as 3rd Earl of Ancaster, 27th Baron Willoughby de Eresby and 4th Lord Aveland.

Gilbert James 3rd Earl of Ancaster, 27th Baron Willoughby de Eresby and 4th Lord Aveland K.C.V.O.

(copy of a painting by John Merton)

*George Horatio 5th Marquess
of Cholmondeley* G.C.V.O.

(from photgraph by C. Beaton)

*The 5th Marquess of Cholmondeley acted as Lord Great Chamberlain for the brief
reign in 1936 of Edward VIII. After the accession of Queen Elizabeth II in 1952 he
acted again until he resigned in favour of his son, later the 6th Marquess, in 1966.
The 6th Marquess acted until his death in 1990 and was succeeded by his son
David, the 7th and current Marquess of Cholmondeley (see frontespiece).*

*George Hugh 6th Marquess of
Cholmondeley* M.C.

(from portrait by John Ward)

CHAPTER V

The Present Co-Holders of the Right to the Office of Lord Great Chamberlain

It has been shown how the right to the office of Lord Great Chamberlain has been divided since the death of the 4th Duke of Ancaster in July 1779, leaving no children but two sisters. The title to the Dukedom passed to his uncle, but lapsed on his death as he had no male heir. The younger of the two sisters of the Duke, Georgiana Charlotte, married the 4th Earl of Cholmondeley. The current (7th) Marquess of Cholmondeley is a direct male descendant of hers, and hence has inherited her one half share of the office. He is the person acting as Lord Great Chamberlain during the current reign.

The elder of the two sisters, Priscilla (Lady Willoughby de Eresby), married Mr Peter Burrell (who became Lord Gwydir) who acted as Lord Great Chamberlain for the latter years of the reign of King George III and the first few months of the reign of King George IV before his own death. The grandson of Lady Willoughby died unmarried in 1870, and his one half share became divided between his two sisters, the elder succeeding to the title of Lady Willoughby de Eresby, the younger marrying Lord Carrington; thus each of these two sisters became entitled to a one quarter share of the right to the office of Lord Great Chamberlain.

The great grandson of this Lady Willoughby de Eresby died in 1983 leaving one daughter (the present Lady Willoughby de Eresby) who has inherited one of the quarter shares.

The position regarding the Carrington quarter share is more complicated due to wartime tragedy. As already described, sadly, when the elder son of Lady Carrington (who was himself created Marquess of Lincolnshire and served as Lord Great Chamberlain in the early part of the reign of King George V) died, he was survived by his five daughters, his only son, Viscount Wendover, having died from wounds received in action in 1915.

Thus, the Carrington one quarter share passed equally to these five daughters; hence they each became entitled to a one-twentieth (5 per cent) share.

These daughters and their heirs are:-

1.   Marjorie Cecilia (m 2nd Baron Nunburnholme). She died in 1968 and her interest passed to her son, Charles John (3rd Baron). He

died in 1974 and the interest passed to his son, Ben Charles (4th Baron). The 4th Baron was born in 1928 and died in 1999 and, as he had no son, his 5 per cent share in the Lord Great Chamberlainship has passed equally to his four daughters (as co-parceners), so each became entitled to a 1¼ per cent interest therein. The four daughters are:-

The Hon. Lorraine Mary Charmian, born 1959
The Hon. Mrs Tatiana Ines Alexandra Dent, born 1960
The Hon. Ysbella, born 1963
The Hon. Mrs Ines Monica Garton, born 1963

2. Alexandra Augusta (m Colonel William Llewellyn Palmer). She died leaving two sons (two other sons predeceased her, leaving no issue). Her 5 per cent interest, therefore, passed to her elder surviving son, Brigadier Anthony Llewellyn Palmer, who died without issue. His younger brother, Charles Timothy Llewellyn Palmer, died in 1978 and the 5 per cent interest passed to this younger brother's eldest son, Julian Neil Llewellyn Palmer, who himself died in 2002, and his interest passed to his son Nicholas.

3. Ruperta (m 7th Earl of Dartmouth). Her one son, Viscount Lewisham M.C., was killed in action at the battle of El Alamein in 1942. Lady Dartmouth died in 1963 leaving five daughters so each inherited in equal shares her 5 per cent interest in the Lord Great Chamberlainship and each therefore took a 1 per cent interest therein. These daughters and their heirs are:-

Mary Cecilia (m Commander N.C.M.Findlay). Lady Mary died in 2003 but had two sons, so her 1 per cent interest passed to the elder of these sons, Jonathan.

Elizabeth (m R.L.Basset). Lady Elizabeth died in 2000 and her 1 per cent interest has passed to her son, Bryan.

Diana (m firstly Hon. John Hamilton-Russell). Lady Diana died in 1970 and her 1 per cent interest passed to her elder son, Colonel James Gustavus Hamilton –Russell.

Barbara (m A. Kwiatkowski). Lady Barbara has four sons, so her 1 per cent interest will pass on her death to the eldest, being Jan Kwiatkowski, who himself has four sons.

Josceline Gabrielle (m Lord Templemore, now Marquess of Donegal). She died in 1998 and her 1 per cent interest passed to her son, the Earl of Belfast.

4. Judith Sydney Myee (m Viscount Bury, later 9th Earl of Albermarle). Lady Bury died in 1928 and her interest passed to her son, Derek William Charles, Viscount Bury (who died in 1968) and his interest passed to his son, Rufus Arnold Alexis, now 10th Earl of Albermarle.

5. Victoria Alexandrina (who married firstly Nigel Walter Legge Bourke). Lady Victoria died in 1966 and her interest passed to her son, Sir Harry Legge Bourke. He died in 1973 and his interest passed to his son, William Nigel Henry Legge Bourke.

The percentage shares of each of the present co-holders of the right to act as Lord Great Chamberlain (and therefore able to appoint a deputy to act as such) are:-

The Marquess of Cholmondeley	50%
The Baroness Willoughby de Eresby	25%
Nicholas Llewellyn Palmer	5%
The Earl of Albermarle	5%
William Nigel Henry Legge Bourke	5%
The Hon Lorraine Mary Charmian Wilson	1¼%
The Hon Mrs Tatiana Ines Alexandra Dent	1¼%
The Hon Ysbella Wilson	1¼%
The Hon Mrs Ines Monica Garton	1¼%
Jonathan Findlay	1%
Bryan Basset	1%
Colonel James Gustavus Hamilton-Russell	1%
Lady Barbara Kwiatkowska	1%
The Earl of Belfast	1%
	100%

CHAPTER VI

The Present Position is Genealogically Incorrect

Chapters I, II and V set out briefly how the present rights to hold the office of Lord Great Chamberlain have arisen, the persons now entitled to share in the holding of such office, and the percentage share each holds.

The position can hardly be regarded as satisfactory, with the right held by so many people and with some holding such a small share. However, this follows from the decision of the Committee for Privileges of the House of Lords on 6th May 1902.

> *That it is the opinion of this Committee that the rights of the co-heiresses who have inherited this office are in the Earl of Ancaster, the Marquess of Cholmondeley and the Earl of Carrington, in whom therefore the right of selection of a deputy vests, subject to His Majesty's approval; that in the event of the said Lords not all agreeing, His Majesty may appoint whom he will for the performance of the duties of the office until they shall agree; and that according to the precedents the person appointed must not be of inferior degree to a Knight.*
>
> *The same was agreed to; and it was ordered that the said Resolution be reported to the House.*

This perpetuated the 1781 decision that the right to the office could be held by more than one person.

Whilst the decision in 1902 was in accordance with the precedent of the 1781 decision, it has left the position in the unsatisfactory state of the right to the office being held by several persons. Indeed, this unsatisfactory position was well set out in a newspaper article in 1953 prior to the Coronation of Queen Elizabeth II under the heading *A Genealogical Absurdity* as follows:

> *The Court of Claims gave its sanction to a well-known genealogical absurdity, when it allowed the claim of Lord Cholmondeley to discharge the office of Lord Great Chamberlain at the coronation. To say this is not to reproach Lord Cholmondeley, who is merely carrying out a family arrangement made necessary by a blunder of the House of Lords in 1781, repeated in 1902, and who will of course serve her Majesty well.*
>
> *It is no reproach to the Court of Claims which no doubt feels debarred from disputing the judgement of the House of Lords,*

especially since the Crown, which has a better right to the office, did not choose to appear. Yet the result is to perpetuate long-standing confusion and make greater confusion probable in the future.

The Lord Great Chamberlain, who has charge of the Palace of Westminster, holds the oldest hereditary office in England. It was granted in 1133 by Henry I to Aubrey de Vere, father of the first Earl of Oxford, and his heirs general. The original muddle came about because sometimes it was allowed to go to the heir male instead of the heir general; and, though heirs male breed heirs male and heirs general heirs general to the end of time, to switch from one mode of tracing the pedigree to the other will soon lead the genealogist to persons who are not heirs of any kind to the grantee. This is what has happened.

Lord Cholmondeley holds the largest share among seven persons who are coheirs of a peer; who was wrongly judged in 1626 to be heir general of an earl; who was allowed the office in 1558 as heir male (to the exclusion of the then heirs general) of Aubrey, the master chamberlain of 1133. The essential error was that of 1558; it was made worse in 1626; it was made flagrant in 1781, when the House of Lords made the preposterous decision that this essentially unitary office could be divided among coheirs. King Henry VIII, faced with the same problem in 1526, made the common-sense decision that a divided succession caused the office to revert to the Crown. It seems to have been by a mere mistake about the facts that it was differently treated at the coronation of Elizabeth I.

The heirs male of Aubrey de Vere became extinct in 1703; of the heirs general – a quite different body from the co-parceners now acknowledged – the senior is the Duke of Atholl. These facts are not in dispute. They were established by the greatest of modern genealogists, Round, and were made unanswerably clear by Geoffrey White in The Complete Peerage a few years ago. They were ignored in 1902, not because the House of Lords had any countervailing argument with them, but from reluctance to vary a decision taken 120 years before.

So now the co-parceners take it in turn, reign-by-reign with a frequency proportioned to their purported holdings, to deputise in the office. In the next generation some of the shares are likely to be reduced to one-hundredth part of the whole. Only the House of Lords can end the anomaly; but may not Henry VIII have been right after all?

Reference is made in this article to the very clear summary of the history of the office of the Lord Great Chamberlain from 1133 by Geoffrey White in Appendix F to Vol. X of *The Complete Peerage*. A briefer summary of the history of the Lord Great Chamberlainship and how the right to the office has devolved since 1133 is set out in Chapter II (see also Appendix D).

The conclusion of Geoffrey White's article is that for a variety of reasons the decisions of the House of Lords have been misguided and the right to the office should either have belonged to the then Duke of Atholl as the heir general of Aubrey de Vere (on the basis that when there were only daughters, the right passed to the eldest), or had reverted to the Crown (on the basis that when there were only daughters the senior had no priority and the right to the office could not be divided). Geoffrey White dismisses entirely the possibility that the office of Lord Great Chamberlain was included in the term 'offices' in the award of 1532 (see details in Appendix D), but the decision in 1902 is that it was so included in the 1532 award and the office has been passed to the present co-heirs on this premise.

It will be seen from a study of all the evidence that the descent of the office, since at least the time of King Henry VIII, has been wrong. Nevertheless, the decision of the House of Lords in 1902 is binding and there is no doubt the right to the office is at present held by the persons set out in Chapter V in the proportions set out therein. This could only be altered by a future decision of the House of Lords or by an Act of Parliament, as will be examined in a later chapter.

CHAPTER VII

The Rights and Duties of The Lord Great Chamberlain

The Lord Great Chamberlain is one of the great Offices of State and hence in this capacity is entitled to perform specific services at a Coronation. Up until (and including) the Coronation of King George IV (1821) the Sovereign slept the night before the Coronation in Westminster Palace, the doors of the bedroom being guarded by the Lord Great Chamberlain. He then had the duty before the Monarch rose of bringing his apparel to him and seeing to his dressing.

The Monarch no longer sleeps in Westminster Palace the night before the Coronation so these particular duties are no longer performed, but the Lord Great Chamberlain is still entitled to his fee of 'forty ells of crimson velvet'.

The Lord Great Chamberlain still has his duties at the Coronation. He carries the gloves and linen used at the Coronation, likewise the sword and scabbard and the gold to be offered by the Sovereign, with the robe royal and the crown, and puts them on him and serves and otherwise is in attendance on the Sovereign that day.

It can be assumed that when the office of Lord Great Chamberlain was granted to Alberic de Vere in 1133, he had overall responsibility for the accommodation of his Sovereign in all his palaces. Over the years, many of the duties were passed on to a deputy who at least by 1539 had become recognised as 'the Lord Chamberlain of the Household'. The Lord Great Chamberlain, however, retained his authority at the Palace of Westminster, probably because this was the meeting place of the Lords and Commons ('the seat of government'), but may have lost any duties direct to the Sovereign (except at Coronations and within the Palace of Westminster) at the time King Henry VIII ceased to reside in the Palace of Westminster and moved to Whitehall.

The control of the Lord Great Chamberlain over the Palace of Westminster was one of overall command. There was a separate office of Keeper of Westminster Palace but this was subordinate and the Lord Great Chamberlain (on behalf of the Sovereign) always had paramount control. The Keepership became merged in the 19th century with the Ministry of Works and this government department became responsible for the upkeep of the fabric of the Palace (subject to the Lord Great Chamberlain's control).

Another official also had an important role in the administration of the House of Lords. This was the Gentleman Usher of the Black Rod ('Black Rod'). The origins of this office go back to the reign of King Edward III and the founding of the 'Most Noble of the Garter'. Black Rod was the usher, bearing a black rod as symbol of his authority, who led the knights in procession and 'kept the doors closed' at their services or feasts. His position in respect of the Knights of the Garter remains today.

By 1522 Black Rod had the additional duty of keeping the doors of Parliament and acting as usher to the House of Lords. His duties as such increased and by 1850 he had a staff of 38. Towards the end of the 19th century more responsibility (and staff) was given to the Lord Great Chamberlain and in 1888 the Lord Great Chamberlain was given full charge of the 'services and custody of the House of Lords'.

The assistant to Black Rod, the Yeoman Usher of the Black Rod, at about that time became secretary to the Lord Great Chamberlain and this position lasted until 1971, although there was a gap of two years (1946-1948) when a separate secretary was appointed. After the alterations to the administration of Parliament had been made by the Harold Wilson government (see below) Black Rod himself in 1971 took over the roles of secretary to the Lord Great Chamberlain.

The duties of the Lord Great Chamberlain increased as the importance of Parliament and its security increased. There is shown in Appendix A a list of the duties of the Lord Great Chamberlain in the Palace of Westminster as set out in 1965; thus prior to 1965 it can be seen that it was quite an onerous office.

Files kept within the House of Lords show that in the early 1960s the Yeoman Usher of the Black Rod, as Secretary to the Lord Great Chamberlain, was in constant touch with him on matters of detail as well as matters of policy. The Secretary would send to the Lord Great Chamberlain a memorandum with a large space on the left-hand side and this would be returned by him with his handwritten comments and instructions on that side.

The advent of a Labour government in 1964 with Harold Wilson as Prime Minister and with a Minister of Works (Charles Pannel) who was keen on giving the House of Commons control of its own House, led to radical changes in the control of the Palace of Westminster and in the responsibilities of the Lord Great Chamberlain.

Negotiations took place between the Government and the Lord Great Chamberlain, with no doubt the Crown being kept informed, and a decision as to the future was announced by the Prime Minister in the House of Commons on 23rd March 1965. (See Appendix B for a copy of the Official Report.) The result was that the control of the accommodation and services in that part of the Palace and its precincts occupied by the House of Commons was vested in the Speaker of that House, with similar control of the area of the House of Lords occupied by them being vested in the Lord

Chancellor as Speaker of that House. The control of Westminster Hall and of the Crypt Chapel was vested in the Lord Great Chamberlain, the Lord Chancellor and the Speaker of the House of Commons jointly (with the Minister of Works being responsible for the day-to-day management). The Lord Great Chamberlain retained his then existing functions on Royal occasions and control of the Queen's robing room, the staircase and ante room adjoining and the Royal Gallery.

No changes in the position have occurred since 1965 except that in practice the administration of the Crypt Chapel (St Mary Undercroft) is in the hands of Black Rod, in addition to his many other duties within the House of Lords.

The Lord Great Chamberlain's responsibility for the 'Royal Rooms' at the Palace of Westminster is in conjunction with his duties when the Monarch visits the Palace of Westminster, particularly when the Monarch opens Parliament in the State Opening. He meets the Monarch on her arrival at the House of Lords and, with his wand of office, precedes her (with the Earl Marshal) in her procession through the Royal Gallery to the House of Lords; the Lord Great Chamberlain to the Monarch's left and the Earl Marshal in front of the Monarch.

In summary, the rights and duties of the Lord Great Chamberlain are:-

1.   The right to perform specified services at a Coronation. These are always the subject of a petition laid before the Committee for Privileges.

2.   Ceremonial duties in the Palace of Westminster on the Monarch visiting the Palace, e.g. The State Opening of Parliament.

3.   The organisation of other great occasions within Westminster Hall. e.g. Lyings-in-State.

4.   The organisation when important Heads of State visit or address the Houses of Parliament, including the meeting of such personages.

5.   Sole responsibility for the Monarch's robing room, staircase and ante room adjoining and the Royal Gallery.

6.   In practice, responsibility for the administration of the Crypt Chapel (the Chapel of St Mary Undercroft).

In performing these duties the Lord Great Chamberlain is ably assisted by Black Rod in his role as Secretary to the Lord Great Chamberlain.

CHAPTER VIII

Westminster Hall

An important part of the Palace of Westminster is the very fine Norman hall which survived the fire of 1834. The Hall has been used for important state occasions, the most recent being the Lying-in-State of the Queen Mother. Monarchs' funerals since King Edward VII (other than King Edward VIII) have included such a Lying-in-State in Westminster Hall, an honour that was also accorded to Sir Winston Churchill.

A very good description of the Hall and its history was included in the *Daily Telegraph* (written by Clive Aslet of *Country Life*) at the time of the Lying-in-State of the Queen Mother. It reads:-

Westminster Hall, one of the few ancient parts of the Palace of Westminster to be preserved after it was rebuilt in the 19th century, is one of the most historic buildings in Europe.

While Edward the Confessor founded Westminster Abbey, Westminster Hall owes its present dimensions to the less saintly figure of William Rufus, William the Conqueror's second son and his successor.

In 1099 William Rufus arrived from France and held court in his new hall for the first time. It must have astonished contemporaries. Then as now, it was 240ft.long and 67ft.6in. wide.

There was no other hall on this scale in England, and probably none in Europe, when it was built.

The strain that this undertaking put on the king's masons can be seen from a serious mistake that they made in aligning the columns and buttresses. Those on the west side are 4ft. adrift from those on the east.

The Norman masons were not able to create a roof to span a hall of this width without the support of aisles, which divided the internal space.

In the late 14th century, Richard II ordered the rebuilding of the roof under the eye of the master carpenter, Hugh Herland. It became the great masterpiece of English medieval carpentry.

Spanning so great a width was a prodigious achievement, which provided a large area of open floor below. Not only is it the largest hammerbeam roof in Northern Europe, but as far as anyone can tell, the first. In time, Westminster Hall would be the court in which sentences of agonising death were passed on the pretender Perkin Warbeck; Henry VIII's chancellor, Thomas More; Protector Somerset and Guy Fawkes of the Gunpowder Plot.

The greatest of all state trials took place here in 1649, when Charles I was condemned to be beheaded.

Later, fashionable society flocked there for the trial of George IV's wife, Queen Caroline, for adultery.

The Hall also acted as a kind of market, with stallholders selling hats, spectacles, nick-nacks and books. At other times, it was a favourable place for picking up shop girls and prostitutes.

It has been shown (in Chapter VII) that there was a separate office of Keeper of the Palace of Westminster, and the boundaries between his duties and the overall control of the Lord Great Chamberlain became somewhat confused. The office of Keeper became merged with that of the Minister of Works (a government minister) and the uncertainty continued. This state of affairs was laid to rest in 1961 when both parties put their claims and arguments to one of the Law Lords (Lord Morton of Henryton) and agreed to accept his decision as arbiter. The ruling not only set out his decision as to 'control', but also confirmed the Hall as an integral part of Westminster Palace.

A copy of Lord Morton's opinion is included as Appendix C, and was to the effect that Westminster Hall was an integral part of Westminster Palace and that the Lord Great Chamberlain (as the Sovereign's personal representative) had paramount control, but each of the parties had a measure of control: the Lord Great Chamberlain by virtue of his office as Governor, and the Minister of Works by virtue of his statutory and other functions in relation to public buildings, and his responsibility for monies voted therefore.

This decision that the Lord Great Chamberlain had paramount control over the Hall (and hence over the rest of the Palace) did not find favour with the government and it was only four years later that the Harold Wilson government arranged for such control to be altered (see Chapter VII). The position then established was that the control of Westminster Hall became vested jointly in the Lord Great Chamberlain, as representing the Monarch, and the Lord Chancellor and Speaker of the House of Commons (on behalf of the two Houses of Parliament), with the Minister of Works being responsible for the day-to-day management.

The present joint control by the Lord Great Chamberlain, the Lord Chancellor and the Speaker of the House of Commons was apparent at the Lying-in-State of the Queen Mother when all three were present at the entrance to the Hall when the funeral procession arrived there and the coffin was brought into the Hall.

CHAPTER IX

The Chapel of St Mary Undercroft
(The Crypt Chapel)

The status of the Chapel of St Mary Undercroft as part of the parish of St Margaret's Westminster was referred to as early as the 14th century. The Abbot and Convent of Westminster had asserted a claim of jurisdiction over the Chapel amongst other Chapels within the Palace and to the 'profits and emoluments thereof', as against a similar claim on the part of the Dean and College of St Stephen. After a protracted quarrel, the matter was finally settled in 1389 at royal request. The substance of the agreement reached in that year was that the Chapels within the Palace of Westminster (together with the houses of those ministering therein) should be exempt from abbatical jurisdiction so long as they were used or occupied by the Dean and Canons and their attendants, although they were still classed as *in parochial Sancte Margarete*. With the dissolution of the College of St Stephen, the buildings would revert to parochial jurisdiction. At the time of the dissolution, this parochial jurisdiction was exercised by the Dean and Chapter of Westminster as Rector of St Margaret.

In 1924 the Archbishop of Canterbury attempted to establish ecclesiastical jurisdiction over the Chapel of St Mary Undercroft.

The question of the Archbishop's jurisdiction over the Chapel was submitted by the Lord Great Chamberlain to the Law Officers of the Crown for their opinion in 1925. The Law Officers found that the Chapel had become secularised during the course of time, that it was now merely a room within a Royal Palace and that no ecclesiastical jurisdiction existed. The Law Officers' report said that 'no ecclesiastical jurisdiction exists in respect of the Crypt Chapel. It is therefore under the sole jurisdiction of the Lord Great Chamberlain, to whom application should be made for permission to use the Chapel for baptisms, weddings etc. Arrangements in connection with the preparation of the Chapel for such ceremonies will be made by the Superintendent of Works.'

As a result of the findings of the Law Officers in 1925, the Archbishop of Canterbury subsequently refused to issue Special Licences for weddings to take place in the Chapel. To overcome this difficulty, the King was asked by the Lord Great Chamberlain to state that the Crypt was to be henceforth 'a private Chapel in the Royal Palace of Westminster to be used solely for Christian religious purposes'. This statement was subsequently made by the King in February 1927.

Thus the King granted a room in his Royal Palace (of Westminster) for Christian religious purposes, which by custom, and to this day, is used for services of marriages, blessings and baptisms of members and officers of both Houses, their sons, daughters and grandchildren.

Hence it is the Monarch's permission that is required to this day, given through the Lord Great Chamberlain (as keeper of the remaining royal apartments in the Palace) for any service, christening or wedding to take place in the Chapel of St Mary Sub Volta (Undercroft).

In 1972, under the 'Westminster Abbey and St Margaret's Westminster Act of Parliament', St Margaret's Church, its churchyard and the whole of the Palace of Westminster (including the Chapel of St Mary Undercroft) was declared to be within 'The Close'. The 1972 Act refers to this area as the 'specified area' and declares that the Chapel of St Mary Undercroft is therefore to be under the same ecclesiastical jurisdiction as The Close, with the Dean as the Ordinary and subject only to the jurisdiction of Her Majesty as Visitor.

Up to the present day, therefore, the Lord Great Chamberlain acts on the understanding that ecclesiastical authority for services in the Chapel of St Mary Undercroft is vested in the Dean of Westminster Abbey and exercised on his behalf by the Rector of St Margaret's Church (the Speaker's chaplain). The Rector also acts in a supervisory and advisory role in regard to the services that take place there.

The only current involvement of the Archbishop of Canterbury is through his issuing of the Special Licence for Marriages within The Close, although he has no ecclesiastical jurisdiction over The Close, as stated earlier

Because the status of the Chapel has been preserved by the 1972 Act of Parliament, and because the present law only allows marriages in the Chapel which are in accordance with the rights of the Church of England, its status could only be altered by a further Act of Parliament.

CHAPTER X

The Future of the Office

Previous chapters have shown that the right to the office of Lord Great Chamberlain is now held between 14 persons, in varying shares, and that this number is likely to increase over the years.

Between them, these 14 persons have to appoint a deputy and this situation has worked satisfactorily for well over a hundred years. Nevertheless, as the number of persons entitled to appoint the deputy increases, and bearing in mind that the decision on such appointments has to be unanimous, it is likely, at some time in the future, that it will not be possible to get such agreement. This may not happen for some years and, indeed, it is understood there is general agreement as to who is likely to be the 'Carrington' nominee to act as deputy in the next reign.

The position may not be so straightforward at the time of the commencement of the next reign thereafter (this, of course, probably to be the reign of Prince William) or at some time during such reign. On the present basis, the 'agreement' between the various families would be that a 'Cholmondeley' nominee acts as deputy for that reign. This causes no problem whilst the current Marquess is living. On his death there would again be no problem if he had a son or if he had no sons if his cousin Charles was living, as he would inherit the Marquessate. The current Marquess's sisters (being the daughters of a Marquess) could also qualify if it was accepted that there is no reason why a female should not act as deputy. However, since the current Marquess, his three sisters and his cousin Charles are all somewhat older than Prince William, the likelihood is that unless the current Marquess or his cousin have sons, the Marquessate will become extinct and, at some time during the reign of Prince William, occasion would arise when there would be no member of the 'Cholmondeley' family who would qualify to act as deputy, since none might be of the rank of knight or higher.

Indeed, two of the Marquess's sisters have sons but unless they were created peers or knighted, they would not qualify to act as deputy under the present rules.

It can be argued that this provision is now outdated and should be ignored, but this would be going against the actual decision of the House of Lords in 1902 'that according to precedents the person appointed must not be of inferior degree to a Knight'.

To change this would need either an Act of Parliament or a new decision from the House of Lords.

The likelihood is that within the next fifty to sixty years, of the current 14 persons and their descendents who would be entitled to a share of the office of Lord Great Chamberlain, only a select few will qualify to act as deputy. It is likely that the only persons who would so qualify would be the holder of the Marquessate of Cholmondeley (if the Marquessate does not become extinct), the holder of the Barony of Willoughby de Eresby, the holder of the Baronetcy of Aird (if not already the holder of the Barony of Willoughby de Eresby), the holder of the title of Earl of Albermarle, and the holder of the title of Marquess of Donegal, or the children of the holder of any such titles. In this context, it is assumed that on the death of the current Lady Willoughby de Eresby, (when the title lapses and goes into abeyance) such title will be brought out of abeyance on the petition of either Mrs Philippi or Sir John Aird. An addition to this list would be if any of the other members married a peer then their children would also qualify, and of course also any other member who was either raised to the peerage or knighted.

The fact that the number of persons so entitled to appoint the Lord Great Chamberlain is increasing and the fact that many of them would not qualify themselves to act as deputy, means the whole future of the office should be looked at.

In view of the number of persons who share the 'Carrington' 25 per cent interest (12 persons) it is understood that it is considered by such persons that their share of the office should revert for all times in the future to the holder of the Carrington title provided that person is by reason of his age and otherwise eligible.

It can be argued that in any case the office is of little practical consequence and an historic anachronism, so it should be abolished. Over the years other such great offices of state such as 'Constable' have disappeared so this one might also disappear. However, the fact that it is such an historic anachronism is a very good reason why it should be retained. It is part of the historic heritage of the country and part of the majesty and splendour that attracts tourists.

A change in the arrangement for the appointment of the deputy could always be forced by one of the persons entitled to a share in the office refusing to agree to any nomination. The 1902 House of Lords decision clearly shows the appointment of a deputy must be unanimous. The actual wording of the decision was 'that in the event of the said Lords not all agreeing His Majesty may appoint whom he will for the performance of the duties of the office until they shall agree'.

At some time in the future this position ought to be followed; i.e. the right to appoint should revert to the Monarch. The basis might be that in making the choice the Monarch would himself select some person who was one of the descendants of the 3rd Duke of Ancaster who died on 12th August 1778. It was, after all, on the death of his son without issue a year later that the right to the office was divided.

Such a change could only be effected by a private Act of Parliament, and probably would only be likely to succeed if a majority of those persons then entitled to the office indicated they were prepared to forego their rights to appoint, and be prepared to assign their share of such rights to the Monarch.

This would maintain the link with the families who are at present entitled to a share in the office and would show a continuing connection with the original appointment of Alberic de Vere in 1133.

THE RIGHTS AND DUTIES OF THE LORD GREAT
CHAMBERLAIN
PRIOR TO 1965

1. The right to perform specified services at a Coronation. These are always the subject of a petition laid before the Committee for Privileges.

2. Ceremonial duties in the Palace of Westminster on the Monarch visiting the Palace, e.g. The State Opening of Parliament.

3. The organisation of other 'great occasions' within the Palace of Westminster, e.g. Lyings-in-State in Westminster Hall, concerts in Westminster Hall.

4. Routine organisation within the Palace of Westminster (including the Houses of Parliament and Westminster Hall) as follows:

    1) Administrative authority of the House of Lords area at all times, and the House of Commons area when not sitting.

    2) Enforcement of all regulations.

    3) Allocation of accommodation (Commons area allocated to the Sergeant at Arms).

    4) Issue of warrants for occupation of residences.

    5) Maintenance of the dignity of Parliament.

    6) Security. Maintained through police and Palace of Westminster custodians, total about 100.

    7) Fire. four Firemen and apparatus.

    8) Organisation of major functions (in conjunction with Ministry of Works for Westminster Hall).

    9) Organisation of registered guides (about 150).

    10) Control of all visitors.

    11) Entertainment of guests.

12) Use of Crypt Chapel.

13) Car parking (a major problem).

14) Press, photography, television, newsreels.

15) Alterations and improvements to the Palace.

16) Maintenance work (in conjunction with the Ministry of Works).

17) Art and decoration.

18) Negotiation of wages etc. for a staff of about 80.

19) Sports and Social Club, Rifle Club.

20) All work not specifically allocated elsewhere.

21) Answering enquiries of all kinds.

22) Presentation of gifts (Mulberry tree, Cromwell's head).

23) Allocation of committee rooms.

APPENDIX B

CONTROL AND CUSTODY OF THE PALACE OF WESTMINSTER

OFFICIAL REPORT (23rd MARCH 1965)

Her Majesty having graciously agreed that the control, use and occupation of the Palace of Westminster and its precincts shall be permanently enjoyed by the Houses of Parliament saving always Her Majesty's Robing Room, the staircase and ante-room thereto adjoining and the Royal Gallery which are to remain under the control of the Lord Great Chamberlain whose hereditary functions on royal occasions shall also be maintained, the Government have decided that:-

1. The Minister of Public Building and Works shall continue to be responsible to Parliament for the fabric of the Palace and subject to Parliament for its upkeep and any extension and alteration thereof and the provision of furnishing, fuel and light therefore.

2. Subject to the reservations specifically made herein to the Lord Great Chamberlain as representing the Queen and the Minister of Public Building and Works, the control of the accommodation and services in that part of the Palace and its precincts now occupied by or on behalf of the House of Lords shall be vested in the Lord Chancellor as Speaker of the House of Lords on behalf of that House.

   Subject as aforesaid the control of the accommodation and services in that part of the Palace and its precincts now occupied by or on behalf of the House of Commons shall be vested in Mr Speaker on behalf of that House.

   The said respective parts are shown on the plans available in the House of Commons Library.

3. The control of Westminster Hall and the Crypt Chapel shall be vested jointly in the Lord Great Chamberlain and in the two Speakers on behalf of the two Houses. Subject thereto the Minister of Public Building and Works shall be responsible for the day-to-day management of Westminster Hall and the Crypt Chapel.

4. The Minister of Public Building and Works shall be responsible, subject to the arrangements made under the next succeeding paragraph, to both Houses for the provision of such custodians and guides as may be necessary for the Palace.

It is recognised that the powers vested as aforesaid in the Lord Chancellor and Mr Speaker on behalf of the House of Lords and House of Commons respectively may be delegated by each House to such Committee or other authority as it may choose and any such Committee or authority may use such agents for such purposes connected with the exercise of the said powers as it may think fit.

It will be for the Speakers of the two Houses to make arrangements for the provision of such police as may be necessary for the Palace.

The co-heirs in whom the hereditary Office of Lord Great Chamberlain is at present vested, that is to say, the Marquess of Cholmondeley, the Earl of Ancaster and the descendants of the late Charles Robert Marquess of Lincolnshire, who have inherited his rights of co-heirship, desire to record their humble obedience to Her Majesty's commands with respect to the future control, use and occupation of the Palace of Westminster.

It is intended that these arrangements shall become effective on 16th April next.

APPENDIX C

1961 OPINION OF LORD MORTON OF HENRYTON

THE LORD GREAT CHAMBERLAIN
AND
THE MINISTER OF WORKS

The question of which my opinion is desired is stated in the Case of the Minister of Works as follows:- Whether the Lord Great Chamberlain or the Minister of Works has the right to control the use of Westminster Hall or, if each has a measure of control, the extent of their respective rights or powers.

The respective claims of the parties are set out in their Cases as follows:-

The Lord Great Chamberlain claims:-

1.   that the Lord Great Chamberlain in the right of his hereditary office is the Governor of the Royal Palace of Westminster and the Sovereign's personal representative in the Palace;

2.   that Westminster Hall is, and always has been, a part of the said Palace;

3.   that it is established by long usage that the Lord Great Chamberlain exercises a paramount jurisdiction over Westminster Hall and, as such governor and personal representative as aforesaid, assumes a direct control over the Hall wherever occasion warrants;

4.   that the office of Lord Great Chamberlain of England is inalienable;

5.   that the rights and duties of the Keeper of the Old Palace of Westminster, insofar as they were connected with Westminster Hall, were subordinate to the said right and authority of the Lord Great Chamberlain who was and is entitled to assume direct control as aforesaid over Westminster Hall, notwithstanding the rights and duties of the Keeper, if any, in connection with Westminster Hall;

6.   that the use of Westminster Hall for any particular purpose is primarily a matter for decision by Her Majesty through the Lord Great Chamberlain, who is the person who should be approached

on each such occasion, unless such proposed use has been made the subject of an Address to Her Majesty by either House of Parliament or of an Order in Council;

7.   save as aforesaid that the Lord Great Chamberlain, being the proper channel of communication through whom all matters concerning the Palace should be be referred, should be consulted whenever the question of Westminster Hall being required for any particular use arises and that such use should not be arranged without the authority or concurrence of the Lord Great Chamberlain either by the Minister of Works or at all.

The Minister of Works claims –

a)   that he has functions of control and management of Westminster Hall by virtue of his general statutory and other functions in relation to public buildings, and his responsibility to Parliament for moneys voted therefore, and also by virtue of the vesting in him of the office of the Keeper of the old and new Palaces of Westminster;

b)   that the Lord Great Chamberlain's jurisdiction in the Palace of Westminster is not exercised by virtue of his hereditary office, but depends on the implied authority and assent of the Crown and the Ministers of the Crown;

c)   that, whatever the basis of the Lord Great Chamberlain's jurisdiction in the Palace of Westminster, that jurisdiction does not extend to Westminster Hall, having regard to the history of the Keepership and to more recent practice, except in respect of any Coronation ceremony held in the Hall.

I have given long consideration to the question already stated in the light of all the documents before me and the authorities referred to therein, and have reconsidered the whole matter after receiving the parties' answers to the questions which I put to their advisers at a meeting on the 6th of June 1961. I think I can best assist the parties by stating my opinion briefly.

1.   The Lord Great Chamberlain's claims 2 and 4 are admitted by the Minister of Works and the arguments presented on his behalf satisfy me that he is the Governor of the Royal Palace of Westminster and the Sovereign's personal representative in the Palace, in the right of his hereditary office as Lord Great Chamberlain. Westminster Hall is an integral part of that Palace, with no physical boundaries between it and the rest of the

Palace, and I find it impossible to hold that there is any distinction, for this purpose, between the Hall and the remainder of the Palace.

2. Each of the parties has a measure of control of Westminster Hall, the Lord Great Chamberlain by virtue of his office as Governor and the Minister of Works by virtue of his statutory and other functions in relation to public buildings and his responsibility for moneys voted therefore.

The Lord Great Chamberlain claims a paramount jurisdiction but not an exclusive one. See paragraph 23 of his Case. In paragraph 2 of his Case he concedes that 'the Minister of Works is responsible, not only for the fabric of Westminster Hall, but also for its day-to-day management and administration', but he puts forward the three special claims 3, 6 and 7 already set out. Claim 5 is a matter of history and need not be further considered.

Claim 3 was further explained by the Lord Great Chamberlain in his written reply to a question which I asked at a meeting on 6th June 1961. The question and answer were as follows:-

'Q.5.   Points 6 and 7 of the Lord Great Chamberlain's Points of Claim are clear and precise, but I find it difficult to put a precise practical meaning upon the words 'paramount jurisdiction' in Point 3 and to the right claimed to 'assume a direct control over the Hall whenever occasion warrants' in Points 3 and 5. Do these claims add anything to claims 6 and 7? If so, how far do the claims go? Does the Lord Great Chamberlain claim to be entitled to take over complete control of the Hall whenever he thinks 'the occasion warrants', ousting the Minister completely so long as the 'occasion exists'? At the moment, it seems to me difficult to reconcile such a claim with the concessions already mentioned.

A. (1) By 'paramount jurisdiction' the Lord Great Chamberlain means that subject to Her Majesty's commands whether given on Government advice or not the Lord Great Chamberlain is the final authority in the Hall as in the remainder of the Palace. Admittedly this authority is very rarely used to override the opinions of other departments interested, decisions invariably being reached by normal methods of conciliation. Nevertheless the Lord Great Chamberlain claims it to himself and he in no way concedes it to the Minister.

(2)   However, it does not follow that the Minister can or would be 'ousted' from his normal routine functions or that the Lord Great Chamberlain claims 'complete' control which phrase implies that the Minister would be so ousted. It is for this reason that the word 'paramount' rather than 'complete' has been used in the Case.

(3) On the other hand, the Lord Great Chamberlain does lay claim to 'direct' control on occasions when the paramount jurisdiction is exercised. These necessarily lead to his being involved in the discussion of many details with numerous authorities including the Ministry. These details are normally settled by discussion and agreement but on the basis that the Lord Great Chamberlain is the final authority. By 'direct control' the Lord Great Chamberlain means that in the exercise of his jurisdiction he has authority to supervise such arrangements as may be necessary for the particular function in question. The degree of supervision necessary largely depends on the type of function, e.g. it is liable to be more detailed where questions of precedence and ceremonial are involved. (See Annexes A and B to the Lord Great Chamberlain's reply.)

(4)   Thus point 3 of the claim does add something to points 6 and 7. It embodies the general principle covering all matters not excepted as being the Minister's normal routine function. It should nevertheless be remembered that on all great occasions in the Hall the Minister is responsible for more than routine functions since his department invariably supplies many of the material amenities.'

In my opinion, Claim 3, as so explained, and also Claims 6 and 7 are well founded.

3.   It is, I think, both unnecessary and undesirable for me to attempt any further expression of opinion as to the respective rights and duties of the parties in the various circumstances which have arisen in the past and may arise in the future.

I hope that the opinions which I have expressed, coupled with the concession already mentioned, will help in the solution of any difficulties which may arise.

If, however, the parties desire any further help from me, I shall do my best to give it.

Morton of Henryton
18.8.61.

APPENDIX D

The legal basis of the present entitlement of the holder of the Office of Lord Great Chamberlain.

The original charter of the grant of the Lord Great Chamberlainship to Alberic de Vere in 1133 by King Henry I was in the following terms (as translated from Latin).

> *Henry, King of England to the archbishops, bishops, abbots, earls, justices, barons, sheriffs and all his faithful subjects appointed throughout England greeting. Know all men forasmuch as I have given and granted to Alberic de Ver and his heirs after him to hold of me and my heirs my chief Chamberlainship of all England in fee and inheritance. Wherefore I will and firmly command that he and his heirs may hold it by hereditary right with all dignities liberties and honours pertaining to it so well freely and honourably as Robert Malet or any other before him or after him even better and more freely and honourably held with the liveries and lodgings of my court which to the office of Chamberlain pertain.*

This charter was ratified and confirmed to Robert (9th Earl) by King Richard II in 1382 and then further ratified and confirmed to John (13th Earl) by King Henry VIII in 1509.

Despite the clear provisions of the original charter which has been properly construed as a grant to heirs general on the death of the 14th Earl, King Henry VIII granted the office to his heir male, the 15th Earl, for life rather than to his three sisters who were his heirs general. There was at that time a continuing dispute between the new Earl and the three sisters which was resolved in 1532 by an award by the King. In this award the King gave the late Earl's 'offices' to the new Earl and it has since been accepted, by the House of Lords, that this rather minor term included so great an office as the Lord Great Chamberlainship. This award was subsequently confirmed by Act of Parliament.

The only logical explanation of this construction of the award is that the King regarded the right to the office to have lapsed and reverted to the Crown, on the basis the right could not be shared between three sisters, and on this basis he could appoint the office as he wished. Indeed King Henry VIII did appoint the office elsewhere from the death of th 15th Earl of Oxford in 1540 (who had held the office 'for life' only). The 16th Earl managed to recover the office for the coronation of Queen Mary in 1553 and held it with his 'heirs general' thereafter.

It can thus be argued that the view of the House of Lords in 1626 and subsequently, despite King Henry VIII appointing the office elsewhere, is that the office was covered by the award and in effect was a new grant of the office to the 15th Earl on similar terms to the original grant to Alberic de Vere and passed to his heirs general, such heirs being as the law was then understood the nearest relatives of the whole blood.

The only extension to the 1626 decision is that in 1781 it was agreed by the House of Lords (on the advice of the Judges) that the office could be held by more than one person and, when it is held by more than one person, such persons must appoint a deputy to exercise the office.

The 1902 House of Lords decision was consistent with these earlier decisions of 1626 and 1781.

APPENDIX E

The Proceedings of the Committee for Privileges of the House of Lords (January–May 1902).

The reference to the Committee for Privileges was to adjudicate on the competing claims for the office of Lord Great Chamberlain at the coronation of King Edward VII.

In fact, by Letters Patent of 28th August 1901, the King had made an *ad interim* appointment of the Marquess of Cholmondeley to the office of Lord Great Chamberlain so he could act at the actual coronation, but without prejudice to the rights of the other claimants. Up until the death of Queen Victoria the office had been filled as deputy by Lord Willoughby de Eresby (Earl of Ancaster) from February 1871. His appointment was made after the death of his uncle, the previous Lord Willoughby de Eresby, without issue but leaving two sisters. At the time of his appointment he had not succeeded to the title of Lord Willoughby de Eresby but held the further title of Lord Aveland. The Willoughby de Eresby title had passed to his mother (on her claim to have it brought out of abeyance) and his appointment was made by his mother and her sister, Lady Carrington, as the heirs general of the previous Lord Willoughby de Eresby.

The proceedings of the Committee for Privileges of the House of Lords in 1902 was to clarify the position, there being four separate claims to the office as set out in Chapter II.

Counsel appeared for all claimants and the Committee sat to hear the claim on 10 days over a period of time. However, the first day merely led to an adjournment, and on the fourth day the Lord Chancellor was ill and could not sit so the proceedings were adjourned. Thus, in effect, the cases for the applicants were made over seven days with the judgement taking the eighth effective day.

Twenty-six peers attended on the Committee at one time or another but the majority only attended for a day or two. Eleven peers attended regularly and these were: the Earl of Morley as Chairman, who sat all eight days; the Lord Chancellor (Lord Halsbury), the Duke of Norfolk, and Viscount Knutsford, all of whom sat for all of the eight days; and seven of the Law Lords as follows: Lord MacNaughton (8), Lord Shand (5), Lord James of Hereford (8), Lord Brampton (8), Lord Lindley (8), Lord Davey (7) and Lord Robertson (8).

It is interesting to note that some of the claimants attended as members of the Committee on some of the days: Earl of Ancaster (3), Marquess of

Cholmondeley (1) and Lord Carrington (2). It must be assumed they attended as observers only, although Lord Carrington is shown as attending on the last day when the final judgement was given.

The arguments made by Counsel for the claimants were lengthy and many documents (some very old and in Latin) were produced. The presentation of the evidence as shown in the official report takes some 242½ pages, whereas the Report of the Committee for Privileges to the House of Lords given by the Lord Chancellor only takes half a page in the following terms:

> *My Lords, I do not think it will be necessary to go through the voluminous evidence in this case, the particulars of which extend far back in our history – as early as the twelfth century; but it certainly appears that the office of Great Chamberlain of England was granted and enjoyed as an hereditary office, to some extent, perhaps, an anomalous office, and partaking of the character of a dignity, and at the same time comprehending in some of its attributes the character of an office of profit.*

> *The primary question for the Committee is whether the office passed to the Earl of Oxford by the award of King Henry VIII and the Act of Parliament confirming the award. Now it must be observed that these documents are capable of bearing the construction that the office passed, and they have received that construction from upwards of three centuries, both in practice and by a resolution of this House. I think, therefore, that the Committee will be justified in declining to consider the construction de novo.*

> *This disposes of the Duke of Atholl's claim. The Duke's claim was held by the Committee of 1783 to be barred by the Statute of Limitations. I am not prepared to say that it ought to be disposed of by this Committee on the same ground; but I think that the previous decision of the Committee of 1625 against it was right, on the grounds that the office was so far an office of profit as to be capable of seisin, and the descent therefore was according to the rule of the common law.*

> *The result is plain, namely, that when this hereditary office descends to females, such persons, if more than one, have a right, subject to His Majesty's approval, to appoint a deputy to execute the said office.*

I think also that if such persons do not all agree, His Majesty may appoint whom he will for the performance of the duties thereof until the co-heiresses shall agree in nominating a person for that situation to be approved by His Majesty and according to the precedents the person appointed must not be of inferior degree to a knight.

The result is that I move your Lordships that this Committee should agree to report to His Majesty that the rights of the co-heiresses who have inherited this office are in the Earl of Ancaster, the Marquess of Cholmondeley, and the Earl Carrington, in whom therefore the right of a selection of a deputy vests, subject of course to the condition above mentioned.

This decision of the House of Lords establishes:

1] The basis of any claim must be based on the award of 1532 and the Act of Parliament confirming it.

2] At the time of the death of the 18th Earl of Oxford his heir general was the nearest heir of the whole blood rather than his sisters of the half blood (although this is not stated in the judgement, it must follow from the decision).

3] That on the death of a holder (or joint holder) of the office leaving females as the heirs general, the right to the office is divisible between such females who then appoint a deputy.

The formal Resolution of the Committee following the speech of the Lord Chancellor is set out in Chapter VI.

It can also be taken from the decision that at no time (since presumably 1532) has the office reverted to the Crown.

Despite the many hours of argument and evidence, the decision does not set out the basis on which the decisions were made except in the briefest terms. It is also interesting to note that whilst the claim of the Duke of Atholl as heir of Lady Latimer is disposed of since her claim predates the award, his claim as heir of Lady Derby is not dealt with at all, although it can be taken that the Committee accepted it was ruled out by the Statute of Limitations.

The Descent of the Lord Great Chamberlainship from Alberic de Vere 1133 - 1666

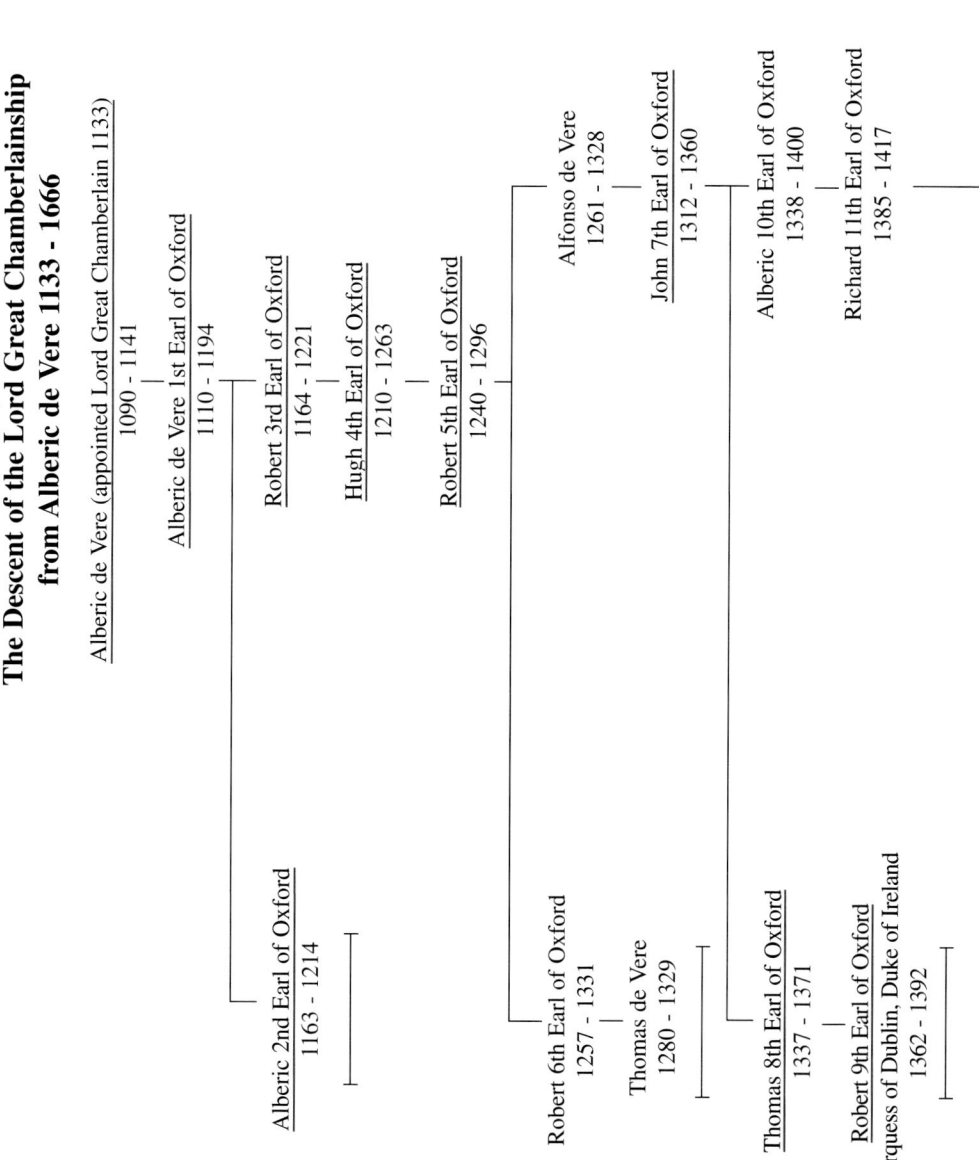

Alberic de Vere (appointed Lord Great Chamberlain 1133)
1090 - 1141

Alberic de Vere 1st Earl of Oxford
1110 - 1194

Robert 3rd Earl of Oxford
1164 - 1221

Hugh 4th Earl of Oxford
1210 - 1263

Robert 5th Earl of Oxford
1240 - 1296

Alfonso de Vere
1261 - 1328

John 7th Earl of Oxford
1312 - 1360

Alberic 10th Earl of Oxford
1338 - 1400

Richard 11th Earl of Oxford
1385 - 1417

Alberic 2nd Earl of Oxford
1163 - 1214

Robert 6th Earl of Oxford
1257 - 1331

Thomas de Vere
1280 - 1329

Thomas 8th Earl of Oxford
1337 - 1371

Robert 9th Earl of Oxford
Marquess of Dublin, Duke of Ireland
1362 - 1392

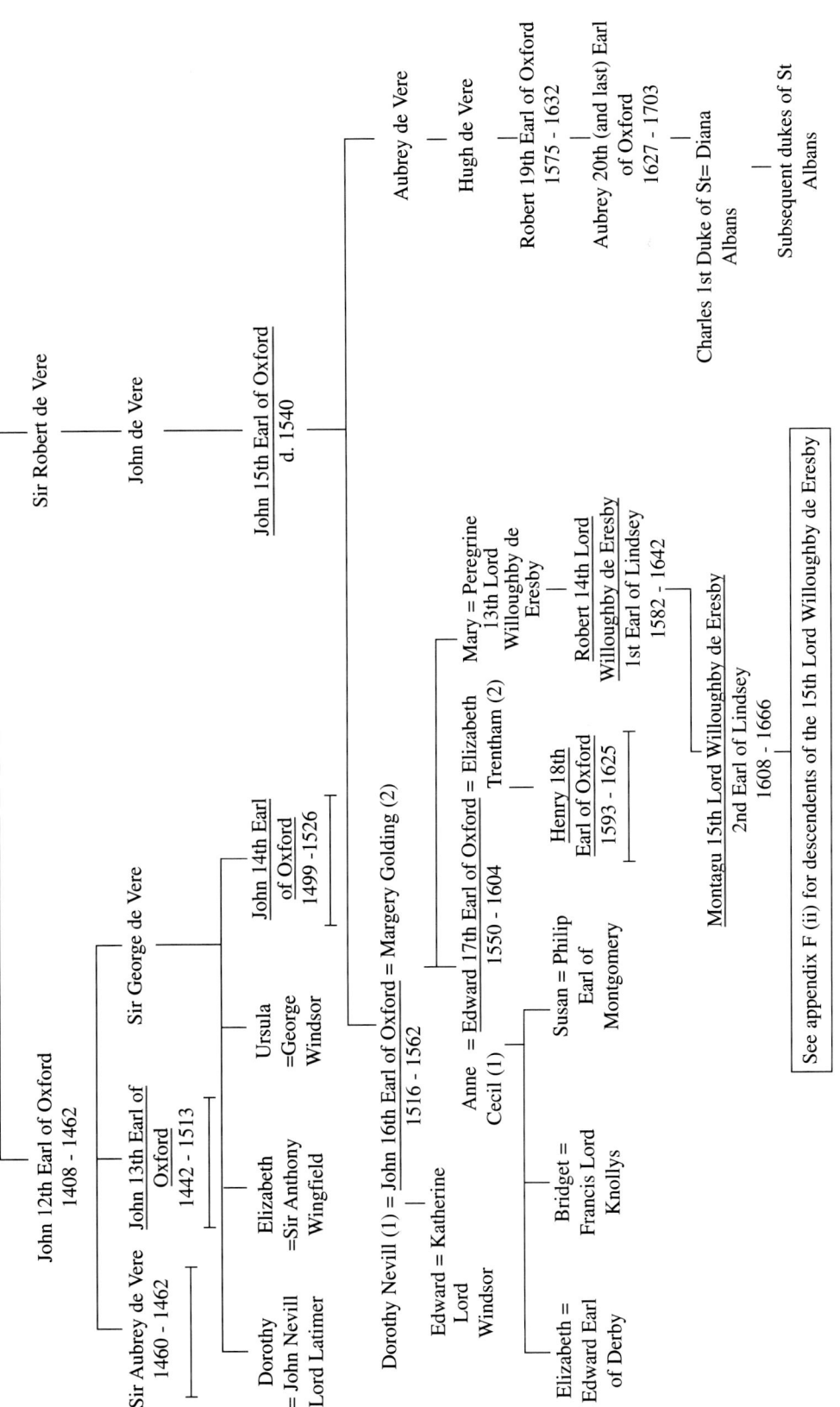

See appendix F (ii) for descendents of the 15th Lord Willoughby de Eresby

APPENDIX F (ii)

Note: The persons who held the office of Lord Great Chamberlain are shown by red underlining

The Descent of the Lord Great Chamberlainship from the death of Montagu 15th Lord Willoughby de Eresby in 1666

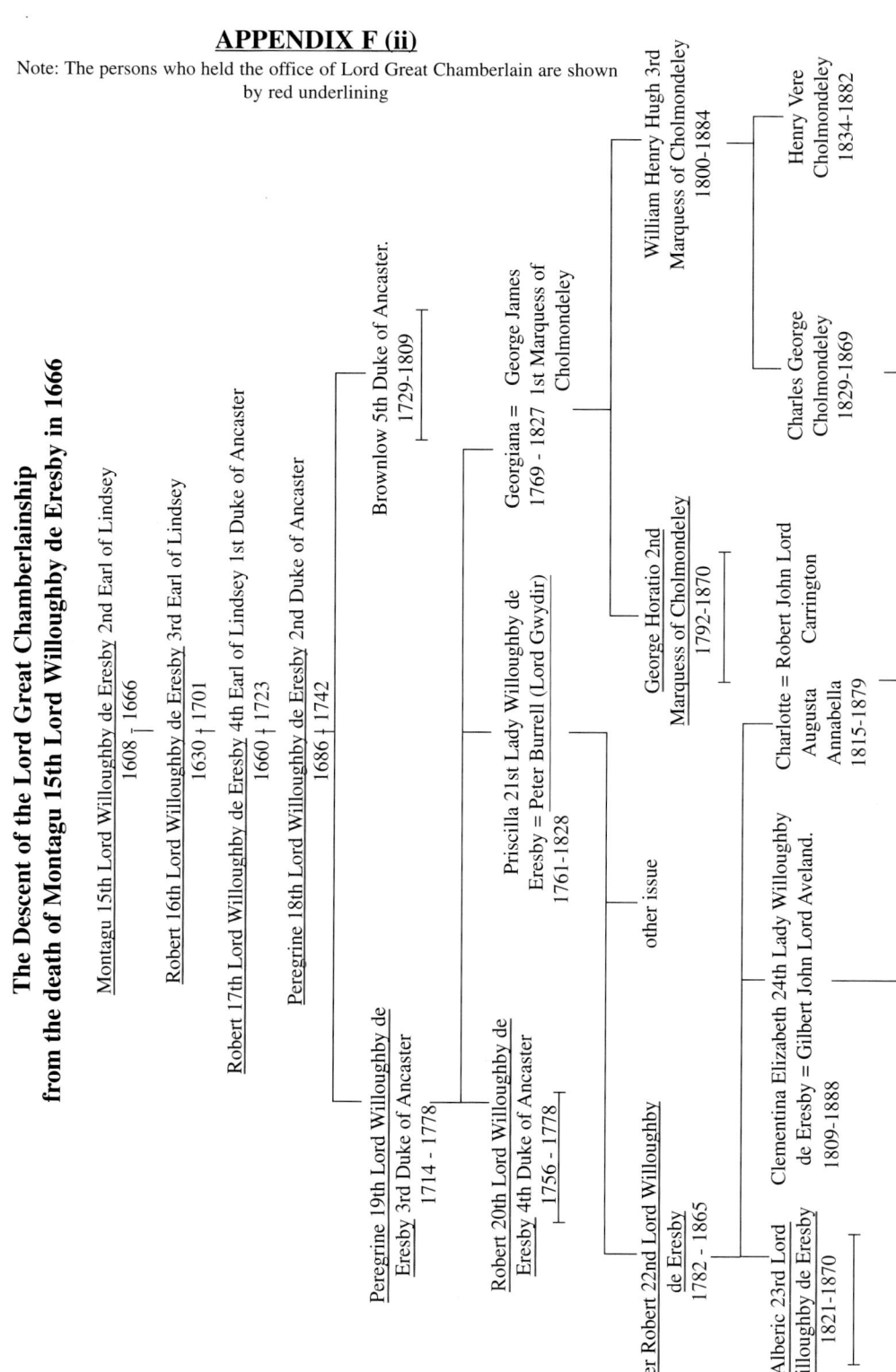

Montagu 15th Lord Willoughby de Eresby 2nd Earl of Lindsey
1608 ⊤ 1666

Robert 16th Lord Willoughby de Eresby 3rd Earl of Lindsey
1630 † 1701

Robert 17th Lord Willoughby de Eresby 4th Earl of Lindsey 1st Duke of Ancaster
1660 † 1723

Peregrine 18th Lord Willoughby de Eresby 2nd Duke of Ancaster
1686 † 1742

Peregrine 19th Lord Willoughby de Eresby 3rd Duke of Ancaster
1714 - 1778

Robert 20th Lord Willoughby de Eresby 4th Duke of Ancaster
1756 - 1778

Brownlow 5th Duke of Ancaster.
1729-1809

Priscilla 21st Lady Willoughby de Eresby = Peter Burrell (Lord Gwydir)
1761-1828

Peter Robert 22nd Lord Willoughby de Eresby
1782 - 1865

Clementina Elizabeth 24th Lady Willoughby de Eresby = Gilbert John Lord Aveland.
1809-1888

Alberic 23rd Lord Willoughby de Eresby
1821-1870

other issue

Georgiana = George James
1769 - 1827 1st Marquess of Cholmondeley

George Horatio 2nd Marquess of Cholmondeley
1792-1870

Charlotte = Robert John Lord Carrington
Augusta Annabella
1815-1879

William Henry Hugh 3rd Marquess of Cholmondeley
1800-1884

Charles George Cholmondeley
1829-1869

Henry Vere Cholmondeley
1834-1882

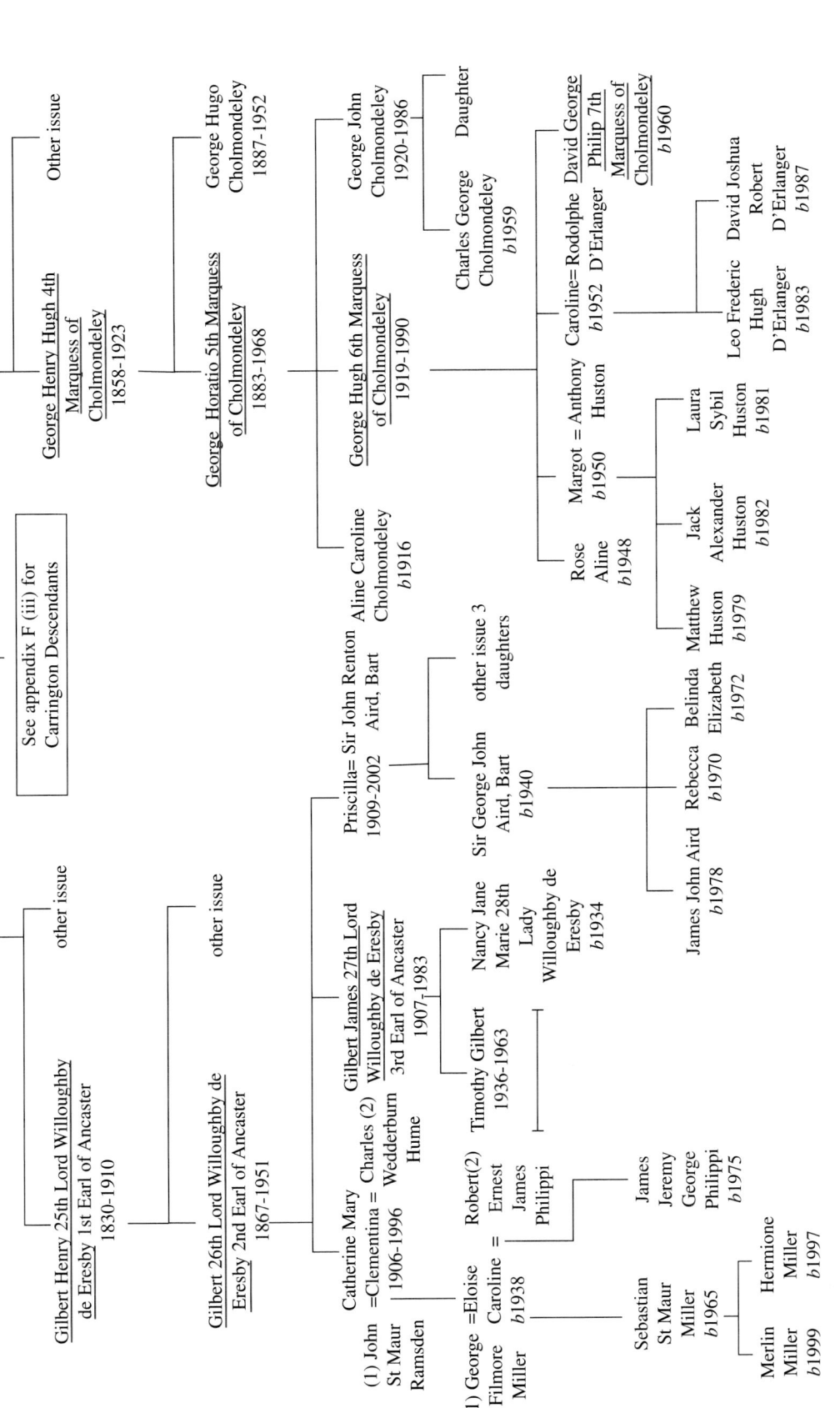

George Henry Hugh 4th
Marquess of
Cholmondeley
1858-1923

Other issue

Gilbert Henry 25th Lord Willoughby
de Eresby 1st Earl of Ancaster
1830-1910

other issue

See appendix F (iii) for
Carrington Descendants

George Hugo
Cholmondeley
1887-1952

George Horatio 5th Marquess
of Cholmondeley
1883-1968

Gilbert 26th Lord Willoughby de
Eresby 2nd Earl of Ancaster
1867-1951

other issue

George John
Cholmondeley
1920-1986

Daughter

George Hugh 6th Marquess
of Cholmondeley
1919-1990

Aline Caroline
Cholmondeley
b1916

Priscilla= Sir John Renton
1909-2002   Aird, Bart

Catherine Mary   Gilbert James 27th Lord
=Clementina = Charles (2)   Willoughby de Eresby
1906-1996   Wedderburn   3rd Earl of Ancaster
Hume   1907-1983

Charles George
Cholmondeley
b1959

David George
Philip 7th
Marquess of
Cholmondeley
b1960

Caroline=Rodolphe
b1952 D'Erlanger

Margot = Anthony
b1950   Huston

Rose
Aline
b1948

Sir George John
Aird, Bart
b1940

other issue 3
daughters

Nancy Jane
Marie 28th
Lady
Willoughby de
Eresby
b1934

Timothy Gilbert
1936-1963

Robert(2)
Ernest
James
Philippi

(1) John   =Eloise
St Maur   Caroline
Ramsden   b1938

(1) George =Eloise
Filmore   Caroline
Miller   b1938

Leo Frederic
Hugh
D'Erlanger
b1983

David Joshua
Robert
D'Erlanger
b1987

Laura
Sybil
Huston
b1981

Jack
Alexander
Huston
b1982

Matthew
Huston
b1979

Belinda
Elizabeth
b1972

Rebecca
b1970

James John Aird
b1978

James
Jeremy
George
Philippi
b1975

Sebastian
St Maur
Miller
b1965

Hermione
Miller
b1997

Merlin
Miller
b1999

Note: The persons who held the office of Lord Great Chamberlain are shown by red underlining

Family Tree showing the Carrington descendants
of Peter Robert (22nd) Baron Willoughby de Eresby (died 1865)
(Lord Great Chamberlain)

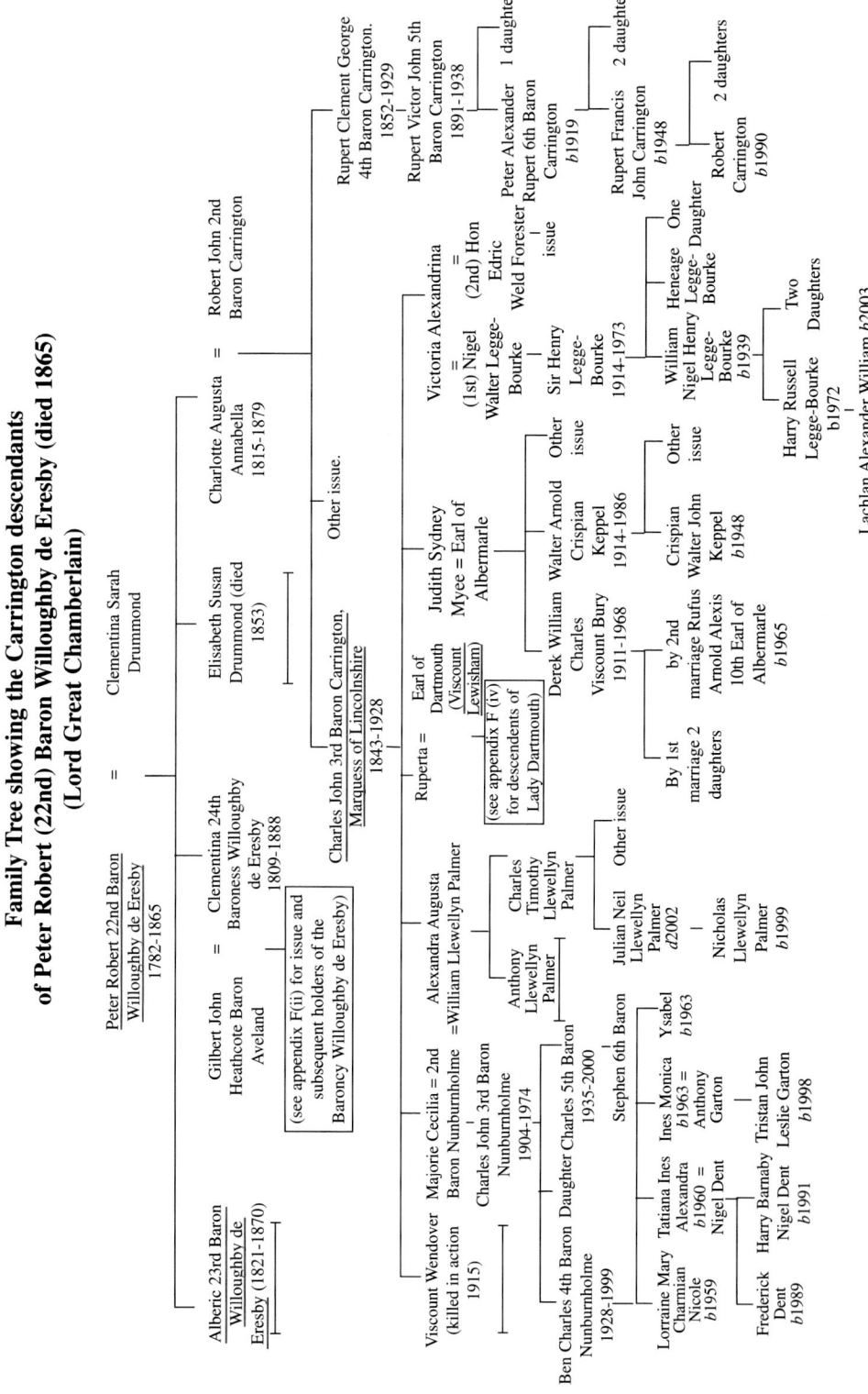

Note: The persons who held the office of Lord Great Chamberlain are shown by red underlining

Family Tree showing the descendants of Lady Dartmouth, daughter of the Marquess of Lincolnshire.

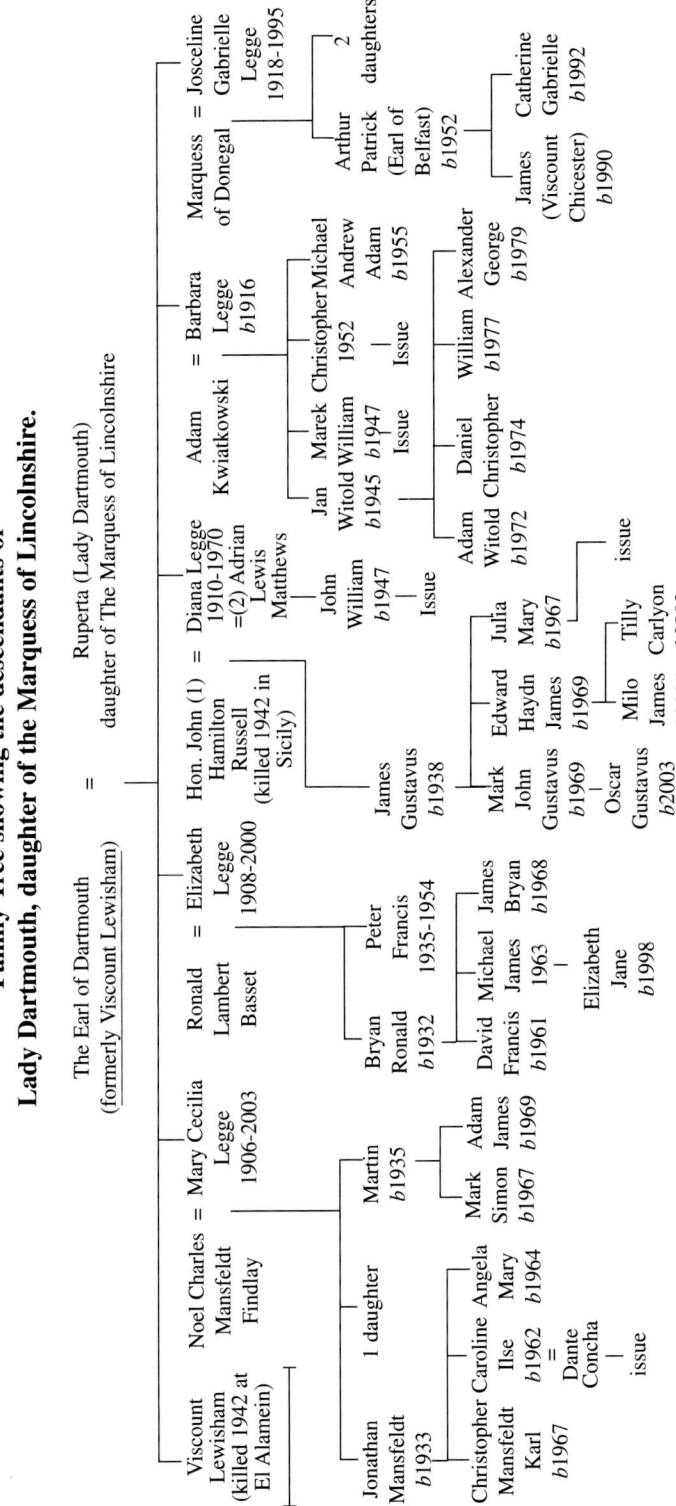

Note: It is likely that there are further great great grandchildren of Lady Dartmouth still to be recorded.

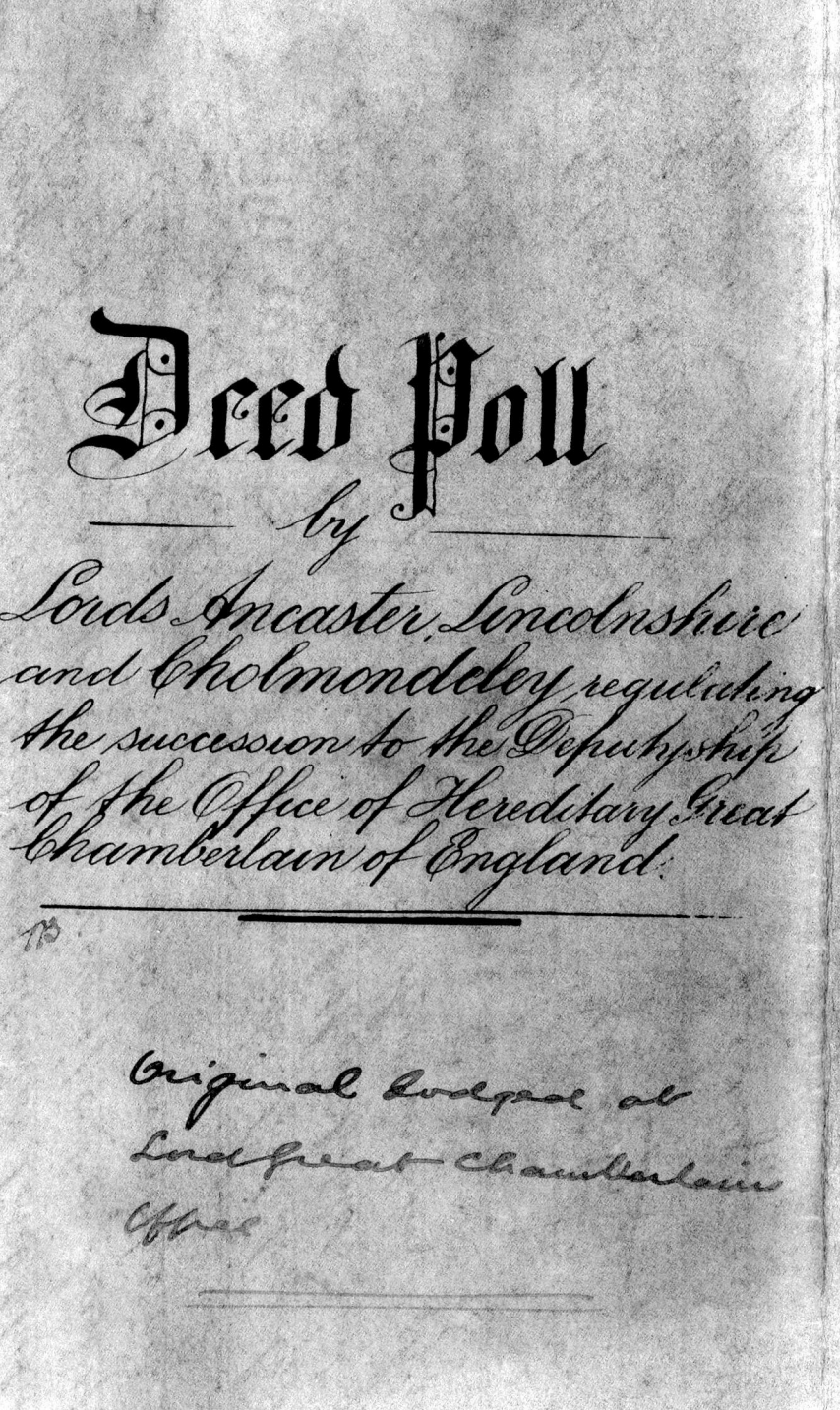

Deed Poll
by

Lords Ancaster, Lincolnshire and Cholmondeley regulating the succession to the Deputyship of the Office of Hereditary Great Chamberlain of England:

Original lodged at Lord Great Chamberlain Office

To all to whom these Presents shall come

The Right Honourable Gilbert Heathcote Drummond-Willoughby Earl of Ancaster Baron Willoughby De Eresby and Baron Aveland (hereinafter called Lord Ancaster) The Most Honourable Charles Robert Marquess of Lincolnshire a Knight of the Most Noble Order of the Garter (hereinafter called Lord Lincolnshire) and The Most Honourable George Henry Hugh Marquess of Cholmondeley (hereinafter called Lord Cholmondeley) Send Greeting Whereas on the sixth day of May One thousand nine hundred and two the Committee for Privileges of the House of Lords resolved that in the opinion of the Committee the rights of the co-heiresses who had inherited the Office of Lord Great Chamberlain of England were in Lord Ancaster Lord Cholmondeley and Lord Lincolnshire (then known and in the said Resolution described as the Earl Carrington) in whom therefore the right of selection of a Deputy vested subject to His Majesty's approval that in the event of the said Lords not all agreeing His Majesty might appoint whom he would for the performance of the duties of the Office until they should agree and that according to the precedents the person appointed must not be of inferior degree to a Knight And whereas said Ancaster derives the rights in him as aforesaid as the heir of The Right Honourable Clementina Elizabeth Baroness Willoughby de Eresby the elder sister of The Right Honourable Charlotte Augusta Annabella Baroness Carington and co-heiress with her of The Right Honourable Alberic Baron Willoughby de Eresby and of The Right Honourable Peter Robert Baron Willoughby de Eresby who was the eldest son and heir of the Right Honourable Priscilla Barbara Elizabeth Baroness Willoughby de Eresby the elder sister of the Most Honourable Georgiana Charlotte Marchioness of Cholmondeley and co-heiress with her of The Most Noble Robert Duke of Ancaster and Kesteven and of The Most Noble Peregrine Duke of Ancaster and Kesteven hereditary Lord Great Chamberlain of England And whereas Lord Lincolnshire derives the right in him as aforesaid as the eldest son and heir of the said Charlotte Augusta Annabella Baroness Carington the younger sister of the said Clementina Elizabeth Baroness Willoughby de Eresby and co-heiress with her of the said Peter Robert Baron Willoughby de

Treaty **And whereas** Lord Cholmondeley derives the rights in him as aforesaid as the great grandson and heir of the said Georgiana Charlotte Marchioness of Cholmondeley the younger sister of the said Priscilla Barbara Elizabeth Baroness Willoughby de Eresby and co-heiress with her of the said Robert Duke of Ancaster and Kesteven and of the said Peregrine Duke of Ancaster and Kesteven **And whereas** by Deed Poll dated the twenty first day of January One thousand nine hundred and eleven and under their hands and seals Lord Ancaster Lord Lincolnshire and Lord Cholmondeley nominated substituted and appointed Lord Lincolnshire to be during the reign of His present Majesty King George V their sufficient Deputy to perform and execute the said Office and such appointment was duly approved by His Majesty King George V **And whereas** Lord Ancaster Lord Lincolnshire and Lord Cholmondeley made the appointment by the said Deed Poll of the twenty first day of January One thousand nine hundred and eleven of Lord Lincolnshire as Deputy to perform and execute the said Office during the reign of His present Majesty King George V in pursuance of an arrangement and understanding with the view to the avoidance of differences and disputes in the future that the said Office should be performed and executed by Lord Ancaster Lord Lincolnshire and Lord Cholmondeley (or their respective heirs) successively as Deputy of all of them during successive reigns as hereinafter provided **Now these Presents witness** and Lord Ancaster Lord Lincolnshire and Lord Cholmondeley do hereby record and declare as follows

1   **The** said Office of Hereditary Great Chamberlain of England with the rank dignity honours duties privileges and profits thereto appertaining shall and may be held exercised and enjoyed (either in person or by deputy) by Lord Ancaster Lord Lincolnshire and Lord Cholmondeley respectively or their respective heirs as deputy of all of them jointly in the order and during the periods hereinafter expressed that is to say

	Person	Period
1	Lord Lincolnshire or his heir	During the reign of His present Majesty King George V
2	Lord Cholmondeley or his heir	During the reign of the next immediate successor to His Majesty King George V
3	Lord Ancaster or his heir	During the reign of the second in succession to His Majesty King George V
4	Lord Cholmondeley or his heir	During the reign of the third in succession to His Majesty King George V
5	Lord Lincolnshire or his heir	During the reign of the fourth in succession to His Majesty King George V

and so on in the same order of succession in the succeeding reigns the intention being that the Deputyship of the said Office shall be held exercised and enjoyed by each of them Lord Ancaster or his heir (or his Deputy as aforesaid) and Lord Lincolnshire or his heir (or his Deputy as aforesaid) once in every four reigns and by Lord Cholmondeley or his heir (or his Deputy as aforesaid) in each alternate reign ————

2 **Nothing** in these presents contained shall prejudice or affect the right of Lord Ancaster Lord Lincolnshire or Lord Cholmondeley or their respective heirs to the entirety or any part or share of or interest in the said Office if such right exists or can either now or at any future date be substantiated ————————

In witness whereof Lord Ancaster Lord Lincolnshire and Lord Cholmondeley have hereunto set their hands and seals the fifteenth day of April One thousand nine hundred and twelve ————

Signed Sealed and delivered }
by the above named Gilbert Heathcote
Drummond-Willoughby Earl of
Ancaster in the presence of

George Davy Ansell
Whissenthorpe, Oakham,
Solr.

Ancaster

Lincolnshire

Cholmondeley

Signed Sealed and delivered }
by the above named Charles Robert
Marquess of Lincolnshire in the
presence of

J. Sed. Jenning's
13 John St. Berkeley Sq. W.
Physician

Signed Sealed and delivered }
by the above named George Henry
Hugh Marquess of Cholmondeley in
the presence of

W. Molesworth Walker
9 Lincolns Inn
Solr.

73

DATED *15th March* . 1966.

D E E D   P O L L

of Appointment of the Honourable
George Hugh Cholmondeley to be
Deputy Hereditary Great Chamberlain
of England during the Reign of
    Queen Elizabeth the Second

KNOW ALL MEN by these PRESENTS that WE THE MOST
HONOURABLE GEORGE HORATIO CHARLES MARQUESS OF CHOLMONDELEY   THE RIGHT
HONOURABLE JAMES HEATHCOTE-DRUMMOND-WILLOUGHBY EARL OF ANCASTER and the
HONOURABLE MARJORIE CECILIA DOWAGER LADY NUNBURNHOLME   VICTORIA
ALEXANDRINA WELD-FORESTER (commonly called Lady Victoria Forester) being
daughters of the late Charles Robert Marquess of Lincolnshire BRIGADIER
ANTHONY LLEWELLEN-PALMER D.S.O. M.C. being a grandson of the said Marquess
of Lincolnshire by his daughter Alexandra Augusta Llewellen-Palmer the
five granddaughters of the said Marquess by his daughter Ruperta namely
MARY CECILIA known as Lady Mary Findlay ELIZABETH known as Lady Elizabeth
Basset DIANA known as Lady Diana Matthews BARBARA known as Lady Barbara
Kwiatkowski and the HONOURABLE JOSCELINE GABRIELLE LADY TEMPLEMORE and
the HONOURABLE DEREK WILLIAM CHARLES KEPPEL(commonly called Viscount Bury)
being a grandson of the said Marquess by his daughter Judith Sydney Myee
Lady Bury being the Persons now together entitled to the Office of the
Hereditary GREAT CHAMBERLAIN OF ENGLAND did by ourselves or our predecessors
in title to the said Office select the said Marquess of Cholmondeley to be
our Deputy during the reign of Her Majesty Queen Elizabeth the Second ___

        A N D   W H E R E A S   the said Marquess of Cholmondeley is desirous
of relinquishing his said Office of Deputy as his execution of these
presents hereby testifies _____

        N O W   T H E R E F O R E   we the parties hereto in conformity with
ancient usage and by virtue of the estate interest power and authority
vested in us do under and by these presents nominate substitute and
appoint the HONOURABLE GEORGE HUGH CHOLMONDELEY (commonly called the Earl
of Rocksavage) in the place of the said Marquess of Cholmondeley to be
during the Reign of Her Majesty Queen Elizabeth the Second our sufficient
Deputy to perform and execute the said Office of Hereditary Great
Chamberlain of England and to exercise and enjoy all such rights and
privileges and do all such acts and perform all such duties and services
as to the said Office do belong and appertain _____

        IN WITNESS whereof the parties hereto have hereunto set their hands
and seals this Fifteenth day of March_____ One thousand nine
hundred and sixty six _____

SIGNED SEALED AND DELIVERED by the)
Said THE MOST HONOURABLE GEORGE   )
HORATIO CHARLES MARQUESS OF   )
CHOLMONDELEY in the presence of :-)   Cholmondeley

SIGNED SEALED AND DELIVERED by the)
said THE RIGHT HONOURABLE JAMES)
HEATHCOTE-DRUMMOND-WILLOUGHBY EARL)
OF ANCASTER in the presence of :-)

Ancaster.

Alan Lee.
Gainsborough. Bourne.
Charterland Land Agent.

SIGNED SEALED AND DELIVERED by the)
said THE HONOURABLE MARJORIE CECILIA)
DOWAGER LADY NUNBURNHOLME in the)
presence of :-)

M. Nunburnholme

Thos. Ratcliffe
45 Elm Park Mansions
Park Walk. SW10

Private Secretary

SIGNED SEALED AND DELIVERED by the)
said LADY VICTORIA ALEXANDRINA)
WELD-FORESTER in the presence of :-)

Victoria Alexandrina
Weld Forester

Marjorie Marshall.
The Laverton House.
Broadway
Housekeeper

SIGNED SEALED AND DELIVERED by the)
said BRIGADIER ANTHONY LLEWELLEN-)
PALMER in the presence of :-)

Anto Llewellen Palmer.

T. H. Radford
Estate Officer
Great Somerford
Chippenham Wilts

SIGNED SEALED AND DELIVERED by the)
said LADY MARY CECILIA FINDLAY in)
the presence of :-)

Mary Cecilia Findlay

Jessie Chisholm
Boyd Lodge
Haremyres

SIGNED SEALED AND DELIVERED by the)
said LADY ELIZABETH BASSET in the)
presence of :-)

Elizabeth Basset

SIGNED SEALED AND DELIVERED by the)
said LADY DIANA MATTHEWS in the)
presence of :-)

Diana Matthews

R. E. Day.
Albrighton Lodge.
Albrighton
House Wife.

SIGNED SEALED AND DELIVERED by the)
said LADY BARBARA KWIATKOWSKI in)
the presence of :-)

Barbara Kwiatkowski

SIGNED SEALED AND DELIVERED by the)
said HONOURABLE JOSCELINE GABRIELLE)
LADY PENTILMORE in the presence of:-)

Josceline Gabrielle Templemore

      ⬤

SIGNED SEALED AND DELIVERED by the)
said HONOURABLE DEREK WILLIAM)
CHARLES KEPPEL in the presence of:-)

      ⬤

APPENDIX J

DATED _____ 23rd October _____ 1990

The Office of Hereditary
Great Chamberlain
of England

Nomination
of
The Seventh Marquess of Chomondeley
as Deputy by the co-Heirs

ALSOP WILKINSON
6 Dowgate Hill
London
EC4R 2SS

(Note: This document was signed in several separate parts)

KNOW ALL MEN BY THESE PRESENTS that WE THE MOST HONOURABLE DAVID GEORGE PHILIP MARQUESS OF CHOLMONDELEY THE RIGHT HONOURABLE NANCY JANE MARIE BARONESS WILLOUGHBY DE ERESBY THE RIGHT HONOURABLE BEN CHARLES BARON NUNBURNHOLME WILLIAM NIGEL HENRY LEGGE-BOURKE of Penmyarth Glanusk Park Crickhowell Powys JULIAN NEIL LLEWELLEN PALMER of Hallyburton Coupar Angus Blairgowrie Perthshire THE HONOURABLE MARY CECILIA FINDLAY commonly called Lady Mary Findlay of 2 South Close The Precincts Canterbury Kent THE HONOURABLE DAME ELIZABETH BASSET DCVO commonly called Lady Elizabeth Basset of 67 Cottesmore Court Stanford Road London W8 THE HONOURABLE BARBARA KWIATKOWSKI commonly called Lady Barbara Kwiatkowski of The Bothy Patshull Park Burnhill Green Wolverhampton Staffordshire THE MOST HONOURABLE JOSCELINE GABRIELLE MARCHIONESS OF DONEGALL COLONEL JAMES GUSTAVUS HAMILTON-RUSSELL of The Brew House Dodmaston Bridgnorth Shropshire and THE RIGHT HONOURABLE RUFUS ARNOLD ALEXIS EARL OF ALBEMARLE being (as appears from the Schedule hereto) the Persons now together entitled to the Office of the Hereditary Great Chamberlain of England in conformity with ancient Usage and by virtue of the Estate Interest Power and Authority vested in us do by these Presents nominate substitute and appoint the said THE MOST HONOURABLE DAVID GEORGE PHILIP MARQUESS OF CHOLMONDELEY in the place of his late father the Most

Honourable George Hugh Marquess of Cholmondeley who died on 13th March 1990 to be during the Reign of Her Majesty Queen Elizabeth the Second our sufficient Deputy to perform and execute the said Office of Hereditary Great Chamberlain of England and to exercise and enjoy all such Rights and Privileges and do all such Acts and perform all such Duties and Services as to the said Office do belong and appertain

IN WITNESS we have to this deed in six parts set our hands and seals this *twenty third* day of *October* 1990

SCHEDULE

The Devolution of the Office of Lord Great Chamberlain of England

(The names of the present co-heirs parties to this deed are distinguished by an asterisk)

1. Immediately before the death of the 1st Marquess of Lincolnshire on 13th June 1928 the office of Lord Great Chamberlain of England belonged as to a one-half share thereof to the 5th Marquess of Cholmondeley as to a one quarter share to the 2nd Earl of Ancaster and as to a one-quarter share to the said Marquess of Lincolnshire

2. The share of the 5th Marquess of Cholmondeley devolved upon successive marquesses and is now vested in the 7th Marquess*

3. The share of the 2nd Earl of Ancaster devolved upon his son the 3rd earl and then upon the latter's daughter the 27th Baroness Willoughby de Eresby*

4. The share of the 1st Marquess of Lincolnshire devolved upon his five daughters as his co-heiresses

4.1 The share of his eldest daughter Marjorie Cecilia the wife of the 2nd Baron Nunburnholme devolved successively upon her son the 3rd baron and upon his son the 4th baron*

4.2 The share of his daughter Victoria Alexandrina devolved upon Sir Henry Legge-Bourke her elder son by her first marriage to Nigel Walter Henry Legge-Bourke and then upon his son William Nigel Henry Legge-Bourke*

4.3 The share of his daughter Alexandra Augusta devolved upon Anthony Llewellen Palmer the elder of her surviving sons and then upon his nephew Julian Neil Llewellen Palmer* the eldest son of his brother Timothy Llewellen Palmer the younger of her surviving sons

4.4 The share of his daughter Judith Sydney Myee the wife of the 9th Earl of Albemarle devolved successively upon her son the Hon Derek William Charles Keppel (Viscount Bury) and her grandson the 10th earl*

4.5 The share of his daughter Ruperta devolved upon her five daughters by the 7th Earl of Dartmouth as her co-heiresses

4.5.1 Lady Mary Cecilia Findlay*

4.5.2 Lady Elizabeth Basset*

4.5.3 Lady Barbara Kwiatkowski*

4.5.4 Josceline Gabrielle wife of the 7th Marquess of Donegall*

4.5.5 The share of her daughter Diana devolved upon James Gustavus Hamilton-Russell* her eldest son by her first marriage to the Hon. John Hamilton-Russell

SIGNED SEALED AND DELIVERED by)
the said THE HONOURABLE MARY)
CECILIA FINDLAY in the)
presence of :-)

Mary Cecilia Findlay

witness signs *Betty Spiller.*

address *1 South Close, The Precincts, Canterbury, Kent.*

occupation *Widow.*

-4-

SIGNED SEALED AND DELIVERED by)
the said THE HONOURABLE DAME)
ELIZABETH BASSET in the)
presence of:-)

Elizabeth Basset

witness signs *A.V. Benson*
address *9, Burward House - 31 Kensington Court*
Married woman *London W8 5BH*

SIGNED SEALED AND DELIVERED)
by the said THE HONOURABLE)
BARBARA KWIATKOWSKI in the)
presence of:-)

Barbara Kwiatkowski

witness signs *Simon Nield*
address *The Coach House, Parsonage, Pednhill Green,*
Much Hadham, SG10 5NB
occupation *Veterinary Surgeon*

SIGNED SEALED AND DELIVERED by)
the said THE MOST HONOURABLE)
JOSCELINE GABRIELLE)
MARCHIONESS OF DONEGALL in the)
presence of:-)

Josceline Gabrielle Donegall

witness signs *B.M. Power.*
address *Arthurstown.*
occupation *Housewife*

The Office of Hereditary
Great Chamberlain of England

PETITION
of

David George Philip
Marquess of Chomondeley

TO THE QUEEN'S MOST EXCELLENT MAJESTY

THE HUMBLE PETITION of THE MOST · HONOURABLE DAVID GEORGE PHILIP MARQUESS OF CHOLMONDELEY

SHEWETH:-

That the Office of Lord Great Chamberlain of England is vested as to a one-half share thereof in your Petitioner as to a further one-quarter share thereof in THE RIGHT HONOURABLE NANCY JANE MARIE BARONESS WILLOUGHBY DE ERESBY as heiress of the late James Earl of Ancaster and as to the remaining one-quarter thereof in the following descendants of Charles Robert Marquess of Lincolnshire viz THE RIGHT HONOURABLE BEN CHARLES BARON NUNBURNHOLME WILLIAM NIGEL HENRY LEGGE-BOURKE of Penmyarth Glanusk Park Crickhowell Powys JULIAN LLEWELLEN PALMER of Hallyburton Coupar Angus Blairgowrie Perthshire THE HONOURABLE MARY CECILIA FINDLAY commonly called Lady Mary Findlay of 2 South Close The Precincts Canterbury Kent

THE HONOURABLE DAME ELIZABETH BASSET DCVO commonly called Lady Elizabeth Basset of 67 Cottesmore Court Stanford Road London W8 THE HONOURABLE BARBARA KWIATKOWSKI commonly called Lady Barbara Kwiatkowski of The Bothy Patshull Wolverhampton Staffordshire THE MOST HONOURABLE JOSCELINE GABRIELLE MARCHIONESS OF DONEGALL COLONEL JAMES GUSTAVUS HAMILTON-RUSSELL of The Brew House Dodmaston Bridgnorth Shropshire a Colonel in Your Majesty's Army and THE RIGHT HONOURABLE RUFUS ARNOLD ALEXIS EARL OF ALBEMARLE who therefore have the right of selecting a Deputy to exercise the said Office such Deputy to be approved by Your Majesty and according to precedent not to be of inferior degree to a Knight

THAT the Most Honourable George Hugh Marquess of Cholmondeley who had previously exercised the said Office during the Reign of your Majesty died on the Thirteenth day of March One thousand nine hundred and ninety

THAT by an Instrument in several parts dated the *Twenty Nine* day of October One thousand nine hundred and ninety the persons in whom the Office of Lord Great Chamberlain of England is in this Petition shown to be vested did nominate substitute and appoint your Petitioner in place of the late George Hugh Marquess of Cholmondeley to be during Your Majesty's Reign their sufficient Deputy to perform and execute the said Office and to exercise and enjoy all such rights and privileges and do all such acts and perform all such duties and services as to the said Office belong and appertain

-2-

YOUR PETITIONER THEREFORE HUMBLY PRAYS that Your Majesty may be pleased to approve him so nominated substituted and appointed by the said Instrument to be the sufficient Deputy of the parties thereto and to perform and execute the Office of Lord Great Chamberlain of England as before mentioned

AND YOUR PETITIONER WILL EVER PRAY etc.

Cholmondeley